Journey to Easier and Lighter

Faith, Trauma and Healing

Sonya Curtis-Tshuma

Journey to Easier and Lighter

© 2023 Sonya Curtis-Tshuma

All rights reserved. No portion of this book may be reproduced, stored in a retrieval system or transmitted in any form or by any means – electronic, mechanical, photocopy, recording, scanning or other – except for brief quotations in critical reviews or actions, without the prior written permission of the publisher.

Scripture quotations marked (NIV) are taken from the Holy Bible, New International Version®, NIV®. Copyright © 1973, 1978, 1984, 2011 by Biblica, Inc.™ Used by permission of Zondervan. All rights reserved worldwide. www.zondervan.com The "NIV" and "New International Version" are trademarks registered in the United States Patent and Trademark Office by Biblica, Inc.™

Scripture taken from the New King James Version®. Copyright © 1982 by Thomas Nelson. Used by permission. All rights reserved.
Scripture quotations marked (AMP) are taken from the Amplified Bible, Copyright © 2015 by The Lockman Foundation. Used by permission.

Scripture quotations marked (NLT) are taken from the *Holy Bible*, New Living Translation, copyright ©1996, 2004, 2015 by Tyndale House Foundation. Used by permission of Tyndale House Publishers, Carol Stream, Illinois 60188. All rights reserved.

"Scripture quotations taken from the (NASB®) New American Standard Bible®, Copyright 2020 by The Lockman Foundation. Used by permission. All rights reserved. lockman.org"

Dedication

I want to first thank God for giving me the life and the gifts to create this. I thank everyone involved in the project including those who encouraged me when it was just an idea, those who helped to read and edit, and those who helped along in my own journey to an easier and lighter path.

I dedicate this book to Hagar, Dinah and Tamar. Your stories helped me see myself in God's story. I'm thankful scripture doesn't leave the darkness out even if pulpits choose to.

Table of Contents

Introduction	7
Chapter 1 - Wholeness	9
Chapter 2 - Seen	25
Chapter 3 - Self-Image	41
Chapter 4 – Shame	57
Chapter 5 - Safety	71
Chapter 6 - Sharing	93
Chapter 7 - Feelings	113
Chapter 8 - Triggers	133
Chapter 9 – Forgiveness	147
Chapter 10 – Community	167
Afterword	177

Introduction

The hardest part about sharing any part of the past is decentering myself to give the stage to God which is always my goal. I understand that I am a sentence in a never-ending love story where God is the center, the force acting upon all things. I'm a piece of a story that includes biblical women like Hagar and Tamar, and those after them who will need a God to heal what has been broken.

I pray my words undergird the burden of my hope for them well. In writing, I hope to give a face to abuse so we can recognize it could easily affect our daughters, sisters, bosses, or even pastors. And with this awareness, we'll seek consistently to help others along their healing journey.

I desire to make a sensitive topic pulpit and Bible study friendly. I want to give biblical rhetoric to suffering and healing so that we find the courage and the words to speak on it where we haven't, and where we have, we'll discover life-giving language more reflective of God's heart. I want conversations about abuse to be easier to broach and the questions easier to hear especially when we don't have easy answers.

So, whether you're reading this alone or with a group, casually or as a Bible Study, I hope that by the time you reach the end of this Bible Study, you will understand the heaviness of life is not yours to carry alone or forever. Not only are there other women, but ultimately, there is God who can carry it all. I hope to share enough that lightness comes as we redefine strength, safety, and survival. I chose "easier and lighter" because at one point "hard and heavy" described how everything felt in my life. Things looked great on the outside, but external success came at "hard and heavy" price that wasn't making me a better person inside or bringing joy. Matthew 11:28-30 gave me words that changed the trajectory of my life. My prayer is that these words do the same for you.

Chapter 1 - Wholeness

Matthew 11:28-30 (NKJV)
28 Come to Me, all you who labor and are heavy laden, and I will give you rest. 29 Take My yoke upon you and learn from Me, for I am gentle and lowly in heart, and you will find rest for your souls. 30 For My yoke is easy and My burden is light."

Scriptures:

- ☐ Matthew 11:28-30
- ☐ Psalm 39:13-16
- ☐ Isaiah 53
- ☐ John 20:24-7
- ☐ Genesis 1:26-28
- ☐ 1 Corinthians 6:19-20

I wish I better understood wholeness before starting down the path of healing. A childhood scarred by sexual abuse and violence weighed me down. Because of this, I hoped for a road to wholeness that was simple, straightforward, and direct. I thought wholeness meant that one day my past would never affect me—that my emotions would completely disconnect from those memories. I envisioned myself as a woman untouched by trauma: a woman without scars.

The path to wholeness was, in fact, the exact opposite of simple and direct. Instead, the path was like searching for an unnamed city whose location keeps changing– just hoping my heart would recognize peace. Some stops along the way were good days: the joy outweighed the pain, and the laughter distracted from the ache. I thought these days were permanent stops until familiar unrest or a new difficulty sent me searching out a new path. Some stops were in the refuge of women whose path I hoped to follow. But they never showed their scars by sharing what they had overcome. I felt they couldn't lead me where they hadn't gone. So the road to healing started off as a winding path and an unceasing prayer.

I was desperate for a journey that led to a better future. And though I longed to be a woman without scars, scripture introduced me to a Savior that still wore the scars of his torment. This Savior promised me an easier and lighter life (Matthew 11:28-30) while boldly holding out His wounds for me to touch. In His wounds were everything I would need for healing (Isaiah 53:5). I needed this Jesus to make it lighter by taking away those things I didn't need to carry, like shame and guilt. And I needed God to make it easier by strengthening me to carry what I couldn't escape–the memories and the relationships with family members who love both me and my abuser. I trusted Christ to accomplish this promise because His triumph was greater than His suffering. I could relate to His scars even if they didn't entirely make sense.

John 20:24-27 (NIV)
24 Now Thomas (also known as Didymus), one of the Twelve, was not with the disciples when Jesus came. 25 So the other disciples told him, "We have seen the Lord!" But he said to them, "Unless I see the nail marks in his hands and put my finger where the nails were, and put my hand into his side, I will not believe."
26 A week later his disciples were in the house again, and Thomas was with them. Though the doors were locked, Jesus came and stood among them and said,

"Peace be with you!" 27 Then he said to Thomas, "Put your finger here; see my hands. Reach out your hand and put it into my side. Stop doubting and believe."

As I read the gospels, I couldn't understand why Jesus would keep his scars. I mean this is Jesus, who raised the dead and healed the sick, walking around with scars on His hands and feet. The same Jesus who resurrected, showed off in Hell, showed up in Heaven, and came back to prove He'd done both. This is the Messiah: whole, proven, and yet blemished.

Is it that wholeness doesn't equal the absence of scars? Maybe Jesus kept the scars so Thomas could overcome his doubt and prove their power to signify strength and identity (John 20:24-26). Or maybe they were meant to show that wholeness in a fallen world will never be without scars–the evidence that something has been ripped apart and put together again. The Bible describes us as being knit together in the womb (Psalm 139:13).

Psalm 139:13-16 (NIV)
13 For you created my inmost being;
   you knit me together in my mother's womb.
14 I praise you because I am fearfully and wonderfully made;
   your works are wonderful,
   I know that full well.
15 My frame was not hidden from you

> when I was made in the secret place,
> when I was woven together in the depths of the earth.
> 16 Your eyes saw my unformed body;
> all the days ordained for me were written in your book
> before one of them came to be.

We all come into this world pieced together by a God skilled enough to show no seams. But trauma can rip us apart by breaking our hearts and spirits, separating our expectations from reality. The mending back together, by God and those who walk with us in this journey, such as friends and therapists, can leave scars. Ultimately, these physical or emotional scars are evidence of our resistance to being completely broken. They are confirmation that we are stronger than what came to destroy us.

If wholeness meant I didn't have to lose my scars, then healing meant I didn't have to be perfect. I was so busy waiting for this perfect version of myself to arrive that I overlooked some significant blessings–moments when God made things easier and lighter. I missed celebrating when nightmares went from often to sporadic, when every frustration didn't trigger memories, or when I first fell in love. I skipped celebrating when shyness became quietness because it was no longer caused by intimidation. I didn't pause to praise God for the me that embraced hugging or could receive a compliment without suspicion. All these moments and more were overshadowed by trying to reach perfection.

I've realized that healing isn't some momentous destination. As I grow into new versions of myself, each version reconciles with my history. This means engaging with the darkest points of my life with the tools I have at that moment. There are tools and truths that I have found as I've gotten older that younger versions of me didn't have the privilege of knowing. And if I'm honest, there's a resilience and hopefulness of my youth that sometimes my older self has to look back to remember. The student, the mother, the wife, and the career woman have all had their days of reckoning with my past. As I reflect, I have seen myself meet that broken child, relate to her, mourn for her, take time to comfort her, and even recognize her strength.

There is no version of me unaffected by trauma that I can ever return to. It's like walking across a bridge crumbling under the pressure of my feet. There is no going back, and to stand still is to succumb to the pressure and fall. The chasm between who I am and who I was is far too wide to ever find again. The only answer is to keep moving forward. That's worth grieving for a moment, but we can't get stuck there. I grieved what could have been– sang a chorus of "what ifs," "maybes," and "should haves." I painted a picture of a life pieced together with the best scenarios, but the truth is that no one gets a perfect life. And to get stuck here is to risk falling into despair because reality will never live up to that fictional world. Instead, I've learned to embrace the opportunity to become a new person who chooses to be made better by every situation I endure.

    I realize that writing these things can be easier than living them, and I have days when disappointments and hardships try to bring up old thought patterns. On these days, when stress starts to overwhelm me, or I start to feel down, I find a downtown city and take a walk. I avoid places with new buildings full of people looking for the newest fad. Instead, I choose the ones with worn-down buildings covered with graffiti or murals and filled with small stores most have never heard of. Every time I walk through one of them, I think about how long the buildings have been around. I think about how time, weather, and modern architectural trends have fought to kill these places, yet they still stand. They are unique locations with their own quirks and their own people. They are rough around the edges but full of treasures that modern downtowns don't offer. "Pieced to Wholeness" is a poem that I wrote on one of these walks as I realized how powerful it was that these communities continue to claim their own space. It has made me more mindful of claiming my own space as authentically as possible.

Pieced to Wholeness

into this world
souls come dismantled,
pieces packed in flesh,
preserved in blood,
purposed for puzzles
whose image is a picture
of divinity

these pieces
processed through sunrise, sunset
and the gravity of circumstance,
smoothed with kisses,
curved with patience,
advanced with knowledge
painted with tradition
and measured against rebellion,
everyone unique and essential
pieced into wholeness,
into God's image

some ending seamless as photos
as if blemishes were removed at
every stage, as if the edges
had never known separation,
as if they came whole into this world

and some end defined by their flaws,
as if the wind angrily crashed
soul and earth together
in the midst of a storm,
as the sun sealed what the rain
had licked into communion

and if i have a choice,
i want to be the latter,
to be that image
that's hurricane kissed

branded by nature
that has lived and existed
and is valued the more
for its unexplainable stance

i want to be that image
that is kept at a distance
to keep hands and time
and cravings from advancement
from touching the wonder that is me

to show forth the hand
of God with its scars
still in place,
a puzzle with gaps
deep enough
for the world to
find refuge in,
chaotic enough
that humanity
can see its reflection,
if only it won't be turned
away from what it represents

this puzzle is incomplete
without dents, without unevenness
and discoloration
without declaration
that fixing it will somehow
take away from the wholeness it
has found, from all that it is,
from all that i am

I am, in many ways, rough around the edges. I don't precisely fit into common standards, so I sometimes devalue what makes me unique. But it's while walking through these spaces, God's voice reminds me of my beauty and wholeness. He reminds me that I hold treasures and that I am treasured.

The Bible says we are made in God's image (Genesis 1:26-28). We carry in us the ability to reflect God's glory and nature. When God created us in His image, I believe He put a unique measurement of each of His qualities to help us accomplish our purpose and destiny. I also believe life experiences cause those qualities to come out of us. Each lesson we learn, and each moment of joy or sadness brings out more of what God used to piece us together. Our unique self is a piece of God that only we can reflect. I previously thought that it was simply my past that made me different. This belief stemmed from an old nature of carrying secrets and believing no one could truly know me. I've realized that even if I hadn't been abused, I'd still be a unique creation of God because we all have artistry to offer the world as image-bearers of God.

This image, scars and all, bears witness to what we have been through. They are any part of our story that we give voice to or show to others. The thing about scars is that although they show evidence of past pain, they no longer carry the same pain level as the initial wound. Touching them and revealing them doesn't hurt as much. For me, many of my poems are scars. Some I wrote when wounds were open and raw, but now they serve as milestones of how far I've come.

There is no common picture of wholeness; the worst thing we can do for abuse survivors is teach that there is. We weren't created to all look alike but simply to be strong enough to carry the spirit in a way that redefines us as temples (1 Corinthians 6:19-20). Thankfully the Spirit abides gently; He can dwell in broken people without further breaking them. The Spirit asks more for willingness than certainty; its strength helps us hold everything together. If we are whole enough to hold God's spirit and act out of it, then we are whole. We can accomplish all God has for us knowing nothing is impossible.

Pray:

God, I pray that you would touch every broken area in my life with your healing power. When I can't see past my pain, show me your scars in solidarity. Remind me that with them comes the promise of your healing. Remind me that you are made strong in my weakness. As I journey towards healing, hold me together until your love makes me whole. Guide my path with love, counsel, and wisdom. When I get stuck, stretch out your hand. When I get lost, send your light. When I get overwhelmed, send your consolation. Help me appreciate every milestone, overcome every obstacle, and take time to enjoy the journey. In Jesus' name, Amen.

Reflect:

What are the scars in your life?
What does wholeness look like for you?
Name something about yourself that reflects an attribute of God.
What activities do you participate in that remind you to value and appreciate yourself?
Looking back, what moments have I missed celebrating?

Chapter 2 - Seen

Genesis 16:13 (NKJV)
13 Then she called the name of the LORD who spoke to her, You-Are-the-God-Who-Sees; for she said, "Have I also here seen Him who sees me?"

Scriptures:

- ☐ Genesis 16
- ☐ Genesis 21
- ☐ Jeremiah 29:11
- ☐ John 11:33-44

Trauma has a way of overcasting our lives. It can cause every good we accomplish to seem drowned out in its shadow and every bad thing to appear all the more sinister as evidence of everything wrong with us. Then we're left questioning how people view us, including God. I believe that God sees me in every moment of my life. But the question of whether or not He is pleased with what He sees has haunted my worship and cast doubt on His love for me. In my safest, happiest moments, I have been seen, fully known in my darkness and light, and loved in the face of it all. When I am certain of how God sees me, it anchors me so I can grow, but when I'm unsure of how God sees me, I wonder if I am worthy of being seen at all.

One of the first steps to healing is settling this question and becoming assured of God's love. Everyone in my life has not seen or acknowledged me in a loving way, but God has without exception. Hagar's life teaches us this truth.

> **Genesis 16:1-15 (NKJV)**
> 16 Now Sarai, Abram's wife, had borne him no children. And she had an Egyptian maidservant whose name was Hagar. 2 So Sarai said to Abram, "See now, the LORD has restrained me from bearing children. Please, go in to my maid; perhaps I shall obtain

children by her." And Abram heeded the voice of Sarai. 3 Then Sarai, Abram's wife, took Hagar her maid, the Egyptian, and gave her to her husband Abram to be his wife, after Abram had dwelt ten years in the land of Canaan. 4 So he went in to Hagar, and she conceived. And when she saw that she had conceived, her mistress became despised in her eyes.

5 Then Sarai said to Abram, "My wrong be upon you! I gave my maid into your embrace; and when she saw that she had conceived, I became despised in her eyes. The LORD judge between you and me." 6 So Abram said to Sarai, "Indeed your maid is in your hand; do to her as you please." And when Sarai dealt harshly with her, she fled from her presence. 7 Now the Angel of the LORD found her by a spring of water in the wilderness, by the spring on the way to Shur. 8 And He said, "Hagar, Sarai's maid, where have you come from, and where are you going?" She said, "I am fleeing from the presence of my mistress Sarai."9 The Angel of the LORD said to her, "Return to your mistress, and submit yourself under her hand." 10 Then the Angel of the LORD said to her, "I will multiply your descendants exceedingly, so that they shall not be counted for multitude." 11 And the Angel of the LORD said to her:

"Behold, you *are* with child, And you shall bear a son. You shall call his name Ishmael, Because the LORD has heard your affliction. 12 He shall be a wild man; His hand shall be against every man, And every man's hand against him. And he shall dwell in the presence of all his brethren."

13 Then she called the name of the LORD who spoke to her, You-Are-the-God-Who-Sees; for she said, "Have I also here seen Him who sees me?" 14 Therefore the

well was called Beer Lahai Roi; observe, it is between Kadesh and Bered. 15 So Hagar bore Abram a son; and Abram named his son, whom Hagar bore, Ishmael.

Hagar was a slave of Abraham's family. God promised Abraham a son, but his wife, Sarah, couldn't give birth. Trying to make the promise happen on their own, Sarah gave him Hagar to impregnate. Every time I hear this story preached, it's about Abraham doubting God's promise or about Sarah's maneuvering. Rarely is it about the harm caused when humanity tries to do naturally what is meant to happen supernaturally. Seldom is its focus on how people become enslaved and cruelly treated in the name of leaders trying to prove that God has chosen them. If we shifted from the traditional focus on Abraham to Hagar, we'd have no choice but to admit that she was abused. We'd have no choice but to fully see Hagar, knowing that historical setting, cultural context, and/or religious titles don't get to rename abuse as anything other than what it is.

What made Hagar invisible to them often makes her invisible to us. She was just a means to an end for Abraham's family and is often seen as merely a background character in a story to modern-day Christians. We, too, can feel invisible when people only focus on the roles we play, the services we give, and whether we please them or not. They can rename abuse as a service to meet their needs and absolve their conscience. They can see everything but our identity, emotions, and desires. And unfortunately, we start to believe that God feels the same way.

Sarah was content as long as Hagar served her household or slept with Abraham like she was told. But after Hagar got pregnant, the Bible says that "Sarah became despised in her eyes" (Genesis 16:4). This angered Sarah, who thought Hagar had no right to be resentful, so she retaliated by treating her harshly. We don't know exactly why Hagar started to despise Sarah. We do know that Hagar was on the verge of birthing a child who would have more freedom and privilege than her. She believed she was birthing the long-awaited heir and possibly felt it shielded her. Perhaps she felt protected enough to allow herself the simplest form of agency by expressing her emotions.

On the path to healing, we can find ourselves on the verge of producing something worthwhile, whether it's a child, professional success, or hope. The idea of these accomplishments can feel motivating enough to risk showing up in ways we haven't before. We begin to see our potential and share our true voice. Everyone won't be happy when this happens. It can shake up our environment and relationships as people are irritated by emotions and perspectives threatening their comfort.

Hagar's situation became so intolerable that she ran away while pregnant and vulnerable. In the midst of the desert, she finds a God who sees her—being seen meant that God was seeing to it that her life was moving towards her purpose and a closer relationship with Him. God instructed her to "return to her mistress" (Genesis 16:8). I always wondered why God sent her back, but I realized that if she ran away, she would have always looked over her shoulder, wondering if someone was coming for her son. She needed to leave when she could be completely free, and that wasn't until the birth of Isaac, 13 years later. When we fear God is idly watching us, hesitant or unable to intervene, we should trust that the exact opposite is true: God is watching to plan our next steps perfectly.

God tells Hagar to name her son Ishmael, which means "God hears." This meant that even though she was in a place of abuse and mistreatment, every time she said her son's name or heard someone say his name, she remembered that God heard her prayers, and an answer was coming. His name was a daily prayer. Ishmael may not have been the heir Hagar expected, but he was evidence that God hears and comforts. Along our path to healing, we should watch for the Ishmaels in our lives. Look for the people and situations that remind us that there's hope for tomorrow, no matter how bad things are now. Look for the miracles that God can birth out of the most challenging situations.

God's watchfulness shows an attentiveness to her needs. He met more than just the immediate need for water but also the unspoken need for a different future. God promised that Ishmael would be a warrior who lived among his own people. She would find family, freedom, and protection in her son's future. We don't have to fear God is watching and waiting for us to mess up so that He can execute punishment, knowing instead that His eyes are upon us to bless us. The Bible says that His thoughts towards us are "for our good and not for disaster, to give us a future and a hope" (Jeremiah 29:11, NLT). We are more to God than just service providers. He's not content with our suffering as long as we worship but desires to minister to our entire person and to transform our lives.

In biblical times, there was a belief that if you saw God, you would die. Hagar was amazed that she was still alive and found it so meaningful that she named God, El Roi, the "God who sees me." She said to herself, "I have seen the God who sees me (Genesis 16:13)." We know that God sees us. But because we haven't seen Him and don't know, we expect to be looked upon with judgement and intimidation. But when we can see Him as the loving, comforting, sustaining God that He is, we can trust ourselves in His sight. We can welcome His gaze and the healing that comes with it. We can offer Him a new name as The One Who Meets Unspoken Needs.

When Hagar is alone and in dire need, she is seen by God, and this brings great consolation. The story lets us know that God heeded her affliction. He recognized she was in pain. He didn't dismiss it or tell her she shouldn't be angry or upset. God seeing her allowed her to feel understood. I believe the same is true for survivors of abuse. We don't want to be seen just to be told we feel too much or too little. There is comfort in the sincere acknowledgment of a person's heart at every step of their journey.

God sees into the depth of our emotions and is touched by our infirmity: He takes on the burden of feeling what we feel until His compassion and healing are released. Empathy is how our Savior could weep with the people who mourned the death of Lazarus while also knowing he was going to resurrect him (John 11:35). He wept because they were hurting at that moment. That moment of pain mattered and wasn't rushed through or dismissed just because healing was coming. If Christ could take the time to weep with them, we should take the time to weep for ourselves and not see it as a discredit to our faith. We can embrace our tears and faith in the sight of God.

The poem, "Baby Girl", was written when I felt that God couldn't possibly see me in a positive light. I felt that God saw someone who wasn't made in His image, someone rejected and abused. I thought He saw only my sin and feared He would rather look away.

Baby Girl

you are the moon,
the blemished crater that dims
your surface is deceptive,
sometimes the clouds they shade
and because man can only see the darkness
some would say they stained,
forced you to move into a cycle of setting
before the sun could counter you
leaving a darkened horizon to get through

as you begin to rain tear drops
showing flashes of anger,
lightning striking where it may,
thunderous voices in the atmosphere
can frighten more than what's really coming,
warning of a storm forcing itself ahead

and you would have nothing to rain
if it wasn't for the raping of body
and mind that lacking hesitation
evaporated and stored defeat,
forming clouds that casts shadows
in the shape of fear, a form of insecurity

so you pray
father remove the stain
that darkens the skies
making every emotion extreme
or numb,
then wonder what kind of God
allows pain and doesn't answer

listen harder,
silence testifies,
darkness holds a secret
greater than the one you keep,
God can't remove

what isn't there,
what never was
you were never stained,
just stalled in progress,
now let the clouds move away,
always pure and beautiful,
an unstained princess,
daughter of a perfected love
always move towards the Son

God's answer to this poem allowed me to understand how God views me. I thought I understood His nature, but I was wrong. Part of that misunderstanding came from constantly feeling like a Hagar when preachers only talked to Sarahs. When I hear sermons, I am sensitive to which character I identify with and how the preacher treats them. I have often mistaken their thoughts of Hagar as God's thoughts of me. Am I someone that God sees? Can I be chosen? Am I just someone to be used by God without concern for my welfare? Is God unconcerned if I'm suffering or being abused?

Stories like Hagar's answered these questions for me about the nature of God. He sees the broken and the outcast. He blesses us and is concerned for our well-being as His sons and daughters. We serve a God that gazes intently upon what others would rather turn away from. Even when others toss us aside, God has a promise and a plan for our lives. He sees the best in us and is pleased to look upon us.

Pray:

God, thank you for seeing me. Help me to trust that your sight is loving. May my testimony glorify you with a new name. Grant me the desires of their heart. Give me the courage to leave unsafe spaces. Meet me in my wilderness and every place of transitions. Comfort me in the unfamiliar with a promise for my future. And may that promise sustain me in the midst of the journey. Give me the strength to endure and not give up. In Jesus' name, Amen.

Reflect:

How does God see you?

When have you felt unseen?

What promise are you moving toward?

Where are the Ishmaels in your life?

What are ways we can be alone with God?

Chapter 3 - Self-Image

Psalm 139:14 (NASB)
14 I will give thanks to You, because I am awesomely and wonderfully *made*; Wonderful are Your works, And my soul knows it very well.

Scriptures:

- ☐ Mark 8:22-25
- ☐ Matthew 13:14-16
- ☐ Isaiah 42:16
- ☐ John 9:1-5
- ☐ Psalm 139:13-18
- ☐ Song of Solomon 4:7

Imago Dei

shine streaks between ash
on the dust of her face
from undried tears
racing to absorption

while she wonders
if it is sin to question the beauty
of God's creation

if it is, she is guilty
awaiting grace or
condemnation
because she can't
reconcile her face
to beauty or her life
to attractiveness

knowing she is God's
creation buffers so much,
only so long
before the voices come again,
the sadness weighs heavy
and her reflection is despised

so she prays
God, clear my eyes
correct my vision
and if only for a moment
can i see myself
through your image,
hear your thoughts
as you created me
while eternities passed
and feel how meticulously
you sketched the first draft?

can i feel the joy
in which you mixed
the colors that shade me
and hold the tools that measured
the height of my stature
and the curve of my body?

can i walk the circles
you walked around me
pacing, patiently checking
every detail, lovingly
smoothing every
rough spot again and again?

can i touch the stencil
that outlined my birthmark
as you signed and marked
your creativity?

show me
the ears and eyes you
discarded that weren't
good enough for me,
the countenances
that didn't fit my personality,
and the faces i was
never meant to make

and finally, if you favor me,
can i watch as you blew breath
into your masterpiece?

can i hear the satisfaction in your
voice as you finished me
and went back to Eve
creating genes that
would make me
exactly as you imagined
when you called me beautiful?

Understanding how God sees us is a significant step towards healing, but this knowledge alone is not enough to transform how we see ourselves. I understood that God loved me, and yet I struggled to accept it. "Imago Dei" was a prayer for a new lens to see myself the way God saw me. I hoped that if I understood how much effort and attention went into my creation, I could see something in myself that darkness couldn't touch–a beginning value that was unchangeable to God. Until I could see it, I knew I would remain blind.

Before I believed that God loved and saw me, I wouldn't have described myself as blind. I just thought I was unworthy and unattractive. Once I believed, I recognized my blindness: I couldn't see what God saw. The Bible talks about blindness as more than the inability to physically see. It also describes people who have eyes but can't see, meaning that we can't always see the truth of God and His nature (Matthew 13:14-16). As a result, we can't always see ourselves in the proper light. Our self-image can be damaged, sometimes slowly, the way vision fades in old age, and other times immediately, like someone unexpectedly turning off the lights. But God promises the blind that He will lead them and give light to see in the book of Isaiah.

Isaiah 42:16 (NKJV)
16 I will bring the blind by a way they did not know;
I will lead them in paths they have not known.
I will make darkness light before them,
And crooked places straight.
These things I will do for them,
And not forsake them.

Throughout scripture, He fulfilled this promise, healing both physical and spiritual sight. One example of Jesus healing a blind person is found in the gospel of Mark.

Mark 8:22-25 (NKJV)
22 Then He came to Bethsaida; and they brought a blind man to Him, and begged Him to touch him. 23 So He took the blind man by the hand and led him out of the town. And when He had spit on his eyes and put His hands on him, He asked him if he saw anything. 24 And he looked up and said, "I see men like trees, walking." 25 Then He put His hands on his eyes again and made him look up. And he was restored and saw everyone clearly.

We don't know how this man became blind, but people speculated about the reason. Many believed his blindness resulted from sin—either his or his parents. This man likely spent his entire life believing that he deserved blindness and that God had marked him as a sinner for everyone to see. Jesus challenged this belief by describing blindness as an opportunity for God to show Himself as the "light of the world" (John 9:1-5, NKJV). Light is meant to overcome the darkness that causes blindness.

I remember how profound the shift from sight to blindness was for me. One day I saw myself as confident, strong, beautiful, and ready to face any challenge, but everything changed after being assaulted. The attractiveness that was once a gift and a strength had suddenly become a vulnerability. I woke up feeling like an imposter, wearing yesterday like a costume, forcing myself to remember lines and social cues: *smile now, make sure you speak, give that hug, shake that hand. Remember your character's backstory; she's happy, friendly, and intelligent.* The act was exhausting, and every day, there'd be a slight slip up in my ability to pretend. Every night, I would find myself unmasked and unwilling to look at the person beneath the disguise.

I blamed myself and hated my reflection. Beauty had become complicated and tied to my sexuality in a way my emotions couldn't untangle. More than anything, I needed to know I was beautiful outside of lustful desires. But it's hard to be grounded in anything, especially truth, in the aftershock of repeated abuse. So the darkness of insecurity covered my eyes, over and over, longer and longer, until I was blind.

How did blindness happen in your life? Was it a traumatic experience like abuse or the habit of comparison that causes so many of us to lose sight of our beauty? Whatever the cause of our blindness, over time, we can become like the blind man: unwilling to seek Jesus for ourselves because we don't think we deserve anything different. We may think we have to figure it out on our own before we go to God. There is a saying that "people won't believe in you until you believe in yourself." But I think that's false. I needed to know God saw me before I could see myself. It's like salvation: I don't have to get everything right before coming to God; I simply come to God, just as I am, knowing He is faultless and willing to change me. In the same way, we can come blind to an all-seeing God whose power can recover our vision.

The blind man in the Bible didn't ask Jesus to restore his sight, but rather he found healing because his community begged Jesus to heal him. Blind people in the Bible were often beggars supported by the community. Looking back, I realize that my blindness affected my community. They didn't receive the best of me, the gifts I had to give, or the value I had to offer. The people who love and care for us desperately want us to see ourselves the way God sees us. There are people in our lives waiting for us to reveal ourselves instead of always holding back.

When we lack the courage to come to Jesus and the strength to ask for change, grace comes along to help us. A grace that causes a community, scripture, or book like this to bring us before God, begging that we finally see the truth. They pray God would open our eyes and transform our self-image. They hope we'll see ourselves positively and never shrink back or hide. They beg God for mercy to affirm our beauty in the face of rejection, mockery, and comparison. They intercede until we trust we are everything we need to be in God.

For me, it was scriptures like, "I am awesomely and wonderfully made" (Psalm 139:14, NASB) or "You are altogether beautiful, my darling; there is no flaw in you" (Song of Solomon 4:7, NIV) that kept dragging my heart before God. For a while, I continued to discount those words as meant for others. In devotion, I found myself alone with these scriptures, pulled away from the crowd like the blind man. It wasn't a crowd of people, but a mind crowded with negative thoughts. These thoughts were much louder than the singular voice of God who offered a better vision of myself. It can be hard to step away from the voices and images we have grown accustomed to measuring our self-worth by. But in solitude with God and His word, we can learn to trust His guidance. It's here in the word and the presence of God that He deposits something of Himself in us.

After leading the blind man away from the crowd, Jesus spits in his eyes. At first glance, to be spit on sounds gross. Nobody would welcome this. But this is Jesus whose blood cleanses and whose wounds heal! Unlike us, there is power in anything that is a part of Him to cleanse whatever it touches. His saliva lets the light into the blind man's eyes. He washed away everything covering this man's sight and blocking out the light. In the same way, God desires to wash away every lie and deception that covers our eyes, so our self-image won't be easily deflated by rough days, harsh words, or delayed dreams.

He then laid His hands on the man's eyes. Healing began as this blind man encountered Jesus' presence. Having a positive self-image grows as our relationship with God grows. As His presence touches us, we grow closer to God. Without this intimacy, separation from God will stall our healing. Without relationship, truth will never take root in our lives. I found intimacy with God through scripture, prayer, and worship. I began to study these scriptures, memorize them, and rehearse them. But the healing process didn't happen overnight.

The reason I chose to highlight the blind man in Mark is that his healing process wasn't immediate. When Jesus asked him about his sight after touching his eyes the first time, the blind man said, "I see men like trees" (Mark 8:24). He boldly let Jesus know that his sight wasn't clear. The man could have thought, *I don't want to disappoint Jesus so I'll tell Him what I think He wants to hear*. In an attempt to not offend Him or question His power, he would have risked being left with a distorted vision. It takes trust to be honest.

God keeps asking us, too. In my own life, I was surprisingly questioned about my vision. On multiple occasions, ministers, who didn't know me, would stop their sermon and call me to altars or pull me to the side after church, saying, "God just wanted me to ask if you know that you are fearfully and wonderfully made." I often responded with a "yes" to avoid awkward and public conversations about my unbelief. The honest answer was no. I didn't know that I was wonderfully made.

What I couldn't say publicly, I knew enough to say privately to God in worship and on my knees. *God, I know what I am supposed to see, but I still don't. I'm holding on to my version of "men like trees." God, I see beauty like danger. I see our differences instead of your likeness; I see my future like my past, which is awful.* I wasn't worried about hurting God's feelings. Stating my reality meant that I trusted Him to make His word a reality. Truth gave God room to work. It allowed God to lay His hands on me again. The second time Jesus laid his hands on the blind man, his sight was healed completely. Eventually, God's touch allowed those scriptures I read to echo from my mouth to my heart to my truth. It began to matter to me that the God who defines beauty calls me beautiful. And just like the blind man found his sight, I could finally see.

beauty's shadow

shadows depend,
like beauty depends,
on the light and the object
on which it is cast

and when i am cast in the light
of waists the size of magazine covers,
it's funny how my waist expands,
how the images in my mirror
change so suddenly

in the moonlight of nights
of imagined conversations,
of responses to the lines of scripts,
my beauty fades and thins
and i am surprised to see anything
of a reflection in the morning

and in the light of
"let's just be friends,"
the light of blurred tears,
again my beauty morphs
into solid shapes,
nothing distinct,
nothing irreplaceable

in the light of solitude,
of chronic nights of no one
knocking at my door,
or a history of last dates
disguised as firsts,
my beauty wrinkles faster
than my wishes can catch up with

these lights, they seem so endless
and i tire of lights
laying me on the ground

casting me in images
that may or may not please,
tired of being labeled

someone's opposite
someone's insecurity
someone's exotica

someone's urban
someone's plain
someone's model

so i'll no longer lay down
for lights that create borders
by showing only my outline
and filling me with darkness

Pray:

God, thank you for making me beautiful in every way. I confess that I am fearfully and wonderfully made. I pray that you help me see myself as you see me. May every lie that has distorted my vision be quieted by your truth. Help me to not compare myself to others. Cause your light to shine in my dark places. May I trust your hand down new roads, new opportunities and in the midst of new graces. In Jesus name, Amen.

Reflect:

Describe your self-image.

Does your self-image align with what the Bible says about you?

How can your inability to see your beauty affect others?

Who can see the beauty in you that you can't see in yourself? What do they say about you?

What are ways that you have been seen/described that don't reflect who you are?

How can Christians bring their blind areas to God?

Do you ever question your beauty?

Chapter 4 – Shame

Isaiah. 54:4 (NKJV)
4 Do not fear, for you will not be ashamed;
Neither be disgraced, for you will not be put to shame;
For you will forget the shame of your youth,
And will not remember the reproach of your widowhood anymore.

Scriptures:

- ☐ 2 Samuel 13:1-20,
- ☐ Isaiah 54
- ☐ Isaiah 9:6-7
- ☐ 1 Chronicles 4:9-10
- ☐ 2 Samuel 14:27
- ☐ Isaiah 61
- ☐ Psalm 37:13

I have a three-year-old son named Jordan. He's one of those toddlers that tries to read facial expressions after he's done something wrong to determine how much trouble he's in. One day, I was in the kitchen preparing a snack on a small plate. He rushed to the counter and grabbed the plate, causing it to fall and break into pieces. I was surprised that it broke, and, in a loud voice, I said, "Jordan, move!" Between the crash, the surprised look on my face, and my tone of voice, it turned out to be too much for my little guy to handle. He immediately burst into tears and sat in his timeout spot. I repeatedly called his name softly, but he turned away, saying "no" between uncontrollable cries and tears. He was expecting more punishment than I intended to give.

The irony is that I wasn't upset. I was more concerned about him hurting himself on the broken pieces and sharp edges of the plate than I was about it falling. I hadn't planned on putting him in timeout. But he had already punished himself–already assumed I was angry and refused to immediately receive my comfort. After cleaning up the mess, I got him to calm down with hugs, kisses, and encouragement to go and play.

During his self-imposed punishment, my son was a picture of shame–the same picture we can find ourselves in. No, we're not crying in a timeout spot, but we are punishing ourselves by refusing to move and grow. We are frozen: caught off guard by life and what seems too much to handle. We assume that others are judging us and that we've disappointed spiritual, societal, and familial expectations. We continuously punish ourselves and refuse to be comforted and liberated. Tamar, in the Bible, is an example of someone becoming frozen. In 2 Samuel 13, we learn that Tamar was raped by her brother, Amnon.

> **2 Samuel 13:10-14,19-20 (NKJV)**
> 10 Then Amnon said to Tamar, "Bring the food into the bedroom, that I may eat from your hand." And Tamar took the cakes which she had made, and brought *them* to Amnon her brother in the bedroom.
> 11 Now when she had brought *them* to him to eat, he took hold of her and said to her, "Come, lie with me, my sister."
> 12 But she answered him, "No, my brother, do not force me, for no such thing should be done in Israel. Do not do this disgraceful thing! 13 And I, where could I take my shame? And as for you, you would be like one of the fools in Israel. Now therefore, please speak to the king; for he will not withhold me from you." 14 However, he would not heed her voice; and

being stronger than she, he forced her and lay with her.

19 Then Tamar put ashes on her head, and tore her robe of many colors that *was* on her, and laid her hand on her head and went away crying bitterly. 20 And Absalom her brother said to her, "Has Amnon your brother been with you? But now hold your peace, my sister. He *is* your brother; do not take this thing to heart." So Tamar remained desolate in her brother Absalom's house.

Tamar wasn't an ordinary woman; she was the daughter of King David. She was royalty, and that came with certain expectations. Shame starts when we believe we have failed expectations. There was societal pressure because she was part of Israel, God's chosen nation. She expected the citizens of Israel to have a higher sense of morality that aligned with God's laws for them. We can feel that way as believers. We are part of the kingdom of God: a group of believers who are supposed to live by a higher standard set by a God who is loving, powerful, and protective of His own. But when we blame ourselves for abuse, we assume that we have disappointed the expectations of God. We believe we didn't live up to the expectation of a pure and innocent life.

For so long, I carried this pressure to always come to God without complaint and stand before other Christians as the walking fulfillment of God's promises. When I couldn't, I felt ashamed. But the thing I love about the Bible is that it shows people in every condition. It fully displays their strengths and weaknesses during their best and worst seasons. The Bible describes people who questioned their faith, acted out of anger and fear, and made faulty assumptions; it shows people like Tamar, whose trauma changed the course of their lives. These people didn't look like God's great promises, yet they still represent God's truth: the world has corruption and evil that He wants to help His children endure and overcome.

I believe that God uses therapy as one of the ways to help us overcome the effects of abuse, but I also felt shame in seeking out counseling. I was told by ministers close to me that a pastor shouldn't need counseling and that there was a bigger problem if prayer and talking to my pastor wasn't enough. How could people look up to me and trust me as a leader if I went to therapy? Unfortunately, this line of thinking puts an additional burden on those trying to heal. The church and God's reputations are not threatened at the threshold of a therapist's office. There is a place for prayer and spiritual deliverance, but there is also a place for counseling. You can't cast out what is emotional, just like you can't counsel what is demonic. Issues of the heart must be brought to the surface and the truth of them faced. When Jesus met people in grief, despair, doubt, or unforgiveness, He comforted, taught, and demonstrated His power to persuade people of the truth. Christ worked to renew their minds. We should never be ashamed to seek help. In the act of seeking, we will find the nature of God that qualifies Him as a wonderful counselor (Isaiah 9:6-7).

We can also fail our personal expectations. Most people have a standard for their lives. We have an idea of who we want to be and what we want our future to look like. And if we're honest, we hope that if we do what's right, good things will return to us. Tamar knew that her brother had taken advantage of her kindness and, no doubt, wondered how she ended up in that situation. She likely felt that she had failed herself–the expectations she set for her future–and misjudged her strength. I know in my own life, I have felt like I let myself down–like there was some sort of wisdom I should have had. Why didn't I know he was capable of it? Why was I alone with him?

What was it about me that attracted his attention? Why didn't it matter that I was family or that I loved him? All these questions left me feeling guilty and condemned.

In addition to our own, family brings another set of expectations. As a daughter of the king and a virgin, Tamar wore a special robe that displayed her status to everyone. The rape meant she could no longer wear that garment, and everyone would know she was no longer a virgin. It would be an embarrassment to her family and bring both judgment and speculation from those around her. Being sexually abused by a family member makes talking about it a complex issue. My family has amazing, generous, and loving people. I admire them; their support and prayers have meant the world to me. But I know that admitting a family member abused me can shine a negative light on them. I don't want to be the source of pain or embarrassment, and that fear made me feel ashamed of what happened and for sharing it. I didn't know what to do with shame. Like Tamar, I wondered where I could take my shame. Would I be like her and keep it all in my heart or could I take it to God? Thankfully, I found God waiting patiently to receive it.

God is concerned about us hurting ourselves on the broken pieces. The anger, bitterness and sorrow that come from abuse can become sharp edges in our lives that hinder growth. The attack on Tamar transformed what she thought was possible for her life. The Bible tells us that she "remained desolate in her brother Absalom's house" (2 Sam 13:20, NKJV). Desolate means she was devastated, isolated and ruined. God wants so much more for us. He doesn't want a moment to destroy our entire lives. He is concerned about the ways abuse continues to affect us. He doesn't want us to give up on our futures.

God calls out to us.

The same way I softly called my son's name is the same way God calls our names. His intent is to show compassion and understanding. If we listen, we can hear Him say it's not our shame to bear. We are free to drop shame at the feet of the person who deserves it–the person who abused us. They were the ones who didn't live up to expectations. We shouldn't carry the guilt or the punishment for their offense. When we put the shame where it belongs, we release ourselves from judgment and fear. We can finally turn our attention to God.

God comforts us.

Absalom, Tamar's brother, tried his best to comfort his sister. He defended her and sought revenge, but it wasn't enough to remove her shame. God also comforts us to get our attention and change our perspective. His love is strong enough to remove our shame. The blessing of mourning is God's consolation. Consolation can't happen from a distance. It's a promise that God will draw close to us. It's a promise that He'll hear us. It's a promise that His presence will touch the wounded areas. His truth about His love for us becomes a salve to place on the wounds allowing them to heal.

God wants us to go.

He wants us to live boldly, take risks, and bet on ourselves. God knows that the bondage of shame must be stretched out to the point of breaking, like a balloon with too much air. As we live out loud, doing the exact opposite of what shame dictates, we begin to conquer it. Jabez's "enlarge my territory" prayer in 1 Chronicles

4:10 was a prayer to overcome the shame of his name, which meant sorrow or pain. He wanted external confirmation of the internal truth that he was more than his name. In Isaiah 54:2 (NKJV), God encourages Israel with the same sentiment when He says, "Enlarge the place of your tent, and let them stretch out the curtains of your dwellings." With shame no longer restraining them, God declares and promises growth. He knows that as we stretch out, we'll forget everything that limits us, and we'll prove wrong the fears in our hearts that God has forsaken us. We'll prove false the boundary sign set up by the enemy to keep us contained. Every success, small or big, challenges shame. Every area of influence is evidence that someone isn't judging us; instead, they admire us. Shame can't exist alongside acceptance or affirmation.

God wants us to play.

Play is about finding and doing what makes us happy, taking every opportunity to laugh and not taking ourselves so seriously. Absalom loved his sister so much that he named his daughter after her (2 Samuel 14:27). I hope she found joy in seeing her niece grow and play. God equips us to play by blessing us in every area of our lives. We serve a God that gives blessings in exchange for ashes, brokenness, and shame (Isaiah 61). Another scripture says that God will give us double for our shame (Isaiah. 61:7). He gives so much that our shame is forgotten amid joy.

As a mother, watching my son play brings me so much happiness. Seeing his joy at the smallest thing or hearing his infectious laughter puts a smile on my face. I've learned that playing is just as important to his development as academic learning. His ability to play shows that he can relate well to others. It also shows his physical development as he takes greater risks, climbs bigger slides and takes some scary looking jumps. I wouldn't want shame to steal that. God delights in our play. And I think the God who laughs in the face of His enemies finds great joy in fighting the burden of shame with His children's play (Psalm 37:13).

What it really comes down to is that we can't bless and punish ourselves at the same time. We've already spent too much time blaming ourselves for another person's actions. Maybe it's time to risk blessing ourselves. Only those who have lived in shame know how scary this can be because it means facing all the fears that shame brought. But freedom is worth it. Shame doesn't have to win.

Pray:

God, help me to push past every boundary that shame has placed in my life. There are times when I have blamed myself for other's actions and I release myself from that blame. Help me to recognize where I am sabotaging my success or shrinking because I fear what others will think. I don't want to resist your comfort or your presence. May I fully accept and affirm myself as your child. You Help me to find rest in you. Give me the freedom to play, laugh and when needed, to rest. In the name of Jesus, Amen.

Reflect:

What are you ashamed of?

How has shame affected your life?

Are there expectations that you don't feel you've lived up to? Are those expectations you need to live up to?

What are ways you can go and play?

Chapter 5 - Safety
Exodus

2 Timothy 1:7

7 For God has not given us a spirit of fear, but of power and of love and of a sound mind.

Scriptures:

- ☐ Exodus 5:20-21
- ☐ Exodus 3:6-8
- ☐ Exodus 13:17-22
- ☐ Exodus 32:1-3
- ☐ Numbers 13:27-33
- ☐ Nehemiah 9:21
- ☐ 2 Timothy 1:7
- ☐ 2 Corinthians 4:8-10

We don't always call it fear, you know, the emotions that hinder our movement from fearfulness to security. These inclinations make us long for the familiar, fight for control or quickly feel abandoned. And while we may not call it fear, I think if we dig somewhere beneath our emotional reflexes and excuses, we'll find a mislabeled desire for safety. As a preacher, I'm guilty of mislabeling the Israelites' motivations as they journeyed from Egypt to the promised land. I characterized them as immature, ungrateful, and short-sighted because they gave God such a hard time. They refused to fight, challenged authority, constantly complained, and accused God of not doing enough, leading to a 40-year delay in reaching the promise. But when I began to look at them with compassion considering their suffering, I could see hints of fear at the center of every wrong decision. They were scared, and I can empathize with the Israelites' reactions because trauma affects how we respond to uncertainty. I know fear doesn't just disappear because the initial cause of it ends, and I recognized the same issues in my own life that made the journey longer than expected.

The Israelites were leaving Egypt, but the trauma they experienced was real and recent. They were enslaved in Egypt for

400 years. They had only known that life – a life of danger, where rulers slaughtered their children, and they worked under brutal conditions. They knew there was a risk in angering their oppressors, so much so that they initially fought against Moses when he wanted to deliver them. They only saw it as risking more danger.

> **Exodus 5:20-21 (NASB)**
> 20 When they left Pharaoh's presence, they met Moses and Aaron as they were waiting for them. 21 And they said to them, "May the Lord look upon you and judge you, because you have made us repulsive in Pharaoh's sight and in the sight of his servants, to put a sword in their hand to kill us!"

It's hard to chase a promise when you're worried about whether you will live to see the end of the day. Their sense of security was shattered. I imagine when God promised the Israelites a bountiful land far away where they could live free, it sounded a little far-fetched. The same thing can happen to us when we experience abuse. There's a certain sense of safety most have growing up, that nothing major will happen to us, and that everything will be ok with wisdom and God. We believe we know who to trust and that the ones we choose to love will give us a lifetime to love them back. But then abuse happens, wisdom fails, loved ones die or leave, and trust is betrayed. Any promise that we can live with our guard down seems unrealistic.

It can be challenging for God to convince us that fear doesn't have to control our lives. After abuse, it can feel like threats of danger are everywhere. By the time I was in high school, the abuse had stopped, but the fear still lingered. At home, I was in the same space where I was traumatized. I walked into the same room, through the same door, and slept in the same bed, like I was living in a museum dedicated to a past whose ghosts were haunting my present. I had to interact with my abuser at family functions. No matter how much time had passed, I couldn't shake what I knew was possible. The rest of the family didn't know what he did to me, but that didn't affect how my emotions shifted when he was around or when family members displayed affection for him. When my family praised him, it stung. When they lauded his accomplishments, it irritated me, and when they defended him, it felt like a betrayal because I felt defenseless. The danger still felt real, and leaving home seemed the easiest answer to escaping everything.

So when I graduated high school, I moved to Georgia to attend college. I hoped that it meant I was leaving a heaviness that I couldn't shake, that I could break free of my insecurities and that I could escape being beholden to what others had become accustomed to. I wanted to give myself a place to transform from an old me to a new me without explaining the change. It was a chance to leave my past somewhere it wasn't constantly in my face. Georgia was meant to be a liberating and brave space for me – my personal promised land.

But that trip, like Israel's, didn't go exactly as planned. My car may have headed for freedom, but somehow my mind still had the same Texas-sized fears I thought I left. Have you ever reached your destination and realized that you don't remember exactly how you got there? Once, I was supposed to drop a friend off on my way to work, but before I knew it, I had passed my intended stop and was at my job instead. Somewhere along my route, my awareness was dulled by the routine of the same turns until my subconscious took over. I said I was going to one place, but my instinct was to go somewhere entirely different.

We can say we are moving towards freedom and promise, but when fear directs our turns, we end up at the wrong destination or circling like the Israelites. The solo pursuit of safety is problematic because the road to growth has turns and streets that don't sound or look safe. It involves taking risks, dealing with conflict, fighting against obstacles, and sometimes feeling uncomfortable. To avoid these things is to lose the chance to fulfill our dreams and live out our purpose. We can miss out on the life that God promised. In Exodus 3, we can see the promise that God made the Israelites.

> **Exodus 3:6-8 (NKJV)**
> 6 Moreover he said, I am the God of thy father, the God of Abraham, the God of Isaac, and the God of Jacob. And Moses hid his face; for he was afraid to look upon God. 7 And the LORD said, I have surely seen the affliction of my people which are in Egypt, and have heard their cry by reason of their taskmasters; for I know their sorrows; 8 And I am come down to deliver them out of the hand of the Egyptians, and to bring them up out of that land unto a good and large land, unto a land flowing with milk and honey; unto the place of the Canaanites, and the Hittites, and the Amorites, and the Perizzites, and the Hivites, and the Jebusites.

Did you notice that when God ends His declaration of the promised land in Exodus 3:8, He says, "Unto the place of the Canaanites, and the Hittites, and the Amorites, and the Perizzites, and the Hivites, and the Jebusites?" People who have never been afraid may have only focused on the promise, but I bet those of us attuned to fear caught the fine print. Did God just promise what belonged to someone else? A place of promise occupied with people who they assume are stronger and better prepared to fight. God's promises are like that sometimes – promises to make us significant in what seems to be an overcrowded field, promises to cause us to thrive where we would be the first, promises that mean facing intimidation, risks, and our own weaknesses if we want to succeed. When God sent Moses to liberate Israel, they may have been headed toward freedom, but it wouldn't come without a fight. Our promises also require the ability to fight and stand our ground. But the willingness to fight can be the first thing to go when we are afraid.

    God wants to restore the fight in us, but He's not blind to what causes trepidation. Here's what most preachers won't tell us– the trip to the promised land was never meant to be as quick as it could. Canaan may have only been a few weeks away when taking a direct route, but God wasn't interested in that route without first strengthening the people's resolve. God had a plan that considered their apprehensions when they first left Egypt.

Exodus 13:17-18 (NKJV)
17 Then it came to pass, when Pharaoh had let the people go, that God did not lead them *by* way of the land of the Philistines, although that *was* near; for God said, "Lest perhaps the people change their minds when they see war, and return to Egypt." 18 So God led the people around *by* way of the wilderness of the Red Sea. And the children of Israel went up in orderly ranks out of the land of Egypt.

God was concerned about their tolerance level for war and conflict. He knew it might cause them to turn around before they saw their final destination. He took them into the wilderness so that they wouldn't see war. How often have we turned away from an opportunity at the initial sight of trouble? Fear can cause us to give up too soon. God wanted to use the wilderness time to prove His power, love, and protection. Before God let them see the promised land, He established His Tabernacle. He established His ability to reign and His responsibility to defend. God was confirming that He meant to dwell with them permanently.

He established the priestly line of Aaron, meaning that He taught them to become worshipers and servants. And daily, God led them by a cloud, and nightly, He led them by fire (Exodus 13:21-

22). He was proving that in every area of their life, He was willing to lead them where they hadn't been before. God was showing that we can trust Him wherever He takes us. The wilderness was meant to be a hiding place for a while. It was an opportunity for the people to learn their strength and trust God's strength when their power wasn't enough.

When they were finally near the promised land, He wanted them to go in boldly. He had hidden them long enough in the wilderness and desired to reveal them as chosen people. There's a big difference between being hidden and hiding. When we are hidden, God uses that time to restore our faith and remind us of His power. He's allowing us time to heal. Hiding, on the other hand, causes us to stop and conceal ourselves when God is telling us to move forward. Hiding causes us to stay longer in fear than necessary. We hide ourselves when we fail to believe God and remain paralyzed by fear. At this point, we are no longer living according to God's will or plan. The Israelites had a chance to come out of hiding when they reached the promised land. They could go in and take the land and receive all the blessings they found in it. Let's see how they responded.

Numbers 13:27-28, 33 (NKJV)
27 Then they told him, and said: "We went to the land where you sent us. It truly flows with milk and honey, and this is its fruit. 28 Nevertheless the people who dwell in the land are strong; the cities are fortified and very large; moreover we saw the descendants of Anak there. 33 There we saw the giants (the descendants of Anak came from the giants); and we were like grasshoppers in our own sight, and so we were in their sight."

They decided to hide. The spies came back sheepishly and described the people as giants in the land. Most of the nation didn't want to fight after hearing their observations. They turned away from the promise out of fear. The Israelites were intent on hiding out in the wilderness instead of moving forward as warriors. Their fear led them to view themselves as insignificant people fighting against giants. Living in fear can cause us to underestimate ourselves and overestimate danger. It's a loss of perspective. I know what it is to assume I'm the most unqualified person in the room. I have watched people who seemed less qualified than me achieve things I didn't even dare to go after. The God who offers more than we can imagine wants us to have the courage to go after more than we think we are capable of.

Their fear caused them to wander in the wilderness for 40 years. That would allow for a whole generation to be born, a generation who wouldn't know slavery and would only know God's provision and protection. They would be in the wilderness, never sick, never lacking, and their possessions never becoming worn down (Nehemiah 9:21). I believe that the infusion of their courage into the Israelites would give them the boost to move forward. For us, this means that to move beyond fear, we must take that time to build new memories on which to act from. We can find strength in the testimonies of others about God's ability to bless. There's a big difference when we operate from the memory of God fighting for us than when we operate from the memory of being slaves. The scale in our mind that motivates towards fear or courage can be tipped towards courage as we continue to add evidence of God's greatness.

We have to remember that the Bible says, "We are more than conquerors" (Romans 8:37, NKJV). I tend to focus on the "more than" to remind people that there's more to life than overcoming difficulties. However, I can't forget that this scripture also means that we must be at least conquerors, strong enough to fight, stand, and defend when needed. We must be strong enough to trust God to win the battles we're willing to fight through. I wrote the poem, *Israelites in the Wilderness,* as I imagined how challenging that time must have been for them wandering for 40 years in the wilderness.

Israelites in the wilderness

it was better in egypt
we knew it, knew it well
were fed,
could mark the days
the fears we knew, could name
and the thought of being slaves
were sometimes forgotten
in our laughter,
in the days when work
was low and feelings high
and family surrounding

we don't know the desert
but You know us
and were afraid
if we saw war, we would
turn back,
how much more
if our path is marked
by burial of those that have died
and footprints
that we, the living and the dead
have made,
anyone would want to go back
not sure why we left,
always think we want freedom
but maybe we can't travel there
maybe every day, when we
only have memories
of egypt's milk and honey,
not ours but still filling our bellies,
maybe that was enough

didn't ask for greatness,
attention has never gone
well for us
at least not before famines

and plagues
and death,
cycles that don't bring
everyone out

and the truth is we fear greatness,
attention, the following
and guidance of a God
who humanity challenges by
challenging your people,
don't you know
we bear your reputation
your name
your wars
and we know you offer
what is greater than
anything in egypt
but in any fear,
there's safety in the familiar

In the wilderness, the people continued to show fear. Moses went to God up in the mountain for 40 days. The people felt abandoned and defenseless. They struggled with constantly needing God to be present to trust him. I'm not talking about just believing God is always with us in our hearts kind of thing. They wanted to see God move and do miracles. They wanted Moses to tell them what God was saying and thinking at every moment. So it didn't go over too well when Moses was with God in the mountains for 40 days.

Exodus 32:1 (NKJV)
32 Now when the people saw that Moses delayed coming down from the mountain, the people gathered together to Aaron, and said to him, "Come, make us gods that shall go before us; for *as for* this Moses, the man who brought us up out of the land of Egypt, we do not know what has become of him."

The people thought Moses and God wouldn't come back to them. Fear can make us feel abandoned in the absence of constant attention, so we test God or people repeatedly, unable to be satisfied. Christians have times when we don't hear from God as often as we would like or don't sense His presence as strongly as we once did. If we're not careful, we can equate this with a lack of love or commitment on God's part. Fear can cause us to quickly think that God has left us and that we are vulnerable to danger. The Israelites' feelings of abandonment caused them to ask Aaron to create a god in the shape of a calf. Overwhelming fear will have us bowing to idols and any promise of security, whether it has our best interest or not. If we are just after safety, we'll settle for relationships that offer no intimacy, love, or mutual affection just to feel secure. When Moses left, they didn't ask Aaron to lead. They would rather have an idol.

Exodus 32:2-4 (NKJV)
2 And Aaron said to them, "Break off the golden earrings which are in the ears of your wives, your sons, and your daughters, and bring them to me." 3 So all the people broke off the golden earrings which were in their ears, and brought them to Aaron. 4 And he received the gold from their hand, and he fashioned it with an engraving tool, and made a molded calf. Then they said, "This is your god, O Israel, that brought you out of the land of Egypt!"

We'll see throughout their time in the wilderness, they questioned God's leadership choices. They wondered why Moses should be the leader, can't God talk to anybody. They wondered if God only chose Aaron and his lineage for the priesthood. They wanted to lead themselves. I think that's the real purpose of idols, to create gods in the image of ourselves. But fear often motivates this desire to rule and fight against leaders. We seek control because we feel safer in our own hands. We don't want to be at the mercy of others. Leaving fear means entering trust and relationships. Maybe that's why when God says He hasn't given us fear, He reminds us that He has given us love (2 Timothy 1:7).

The people used the wealth they had gained from the Egyptians to make their idol. Fear can cause us to forfeit blessings in exchange for a false sense of security. Fear is wasteful. It takes all of our time and resources just to maintain the status quo. We can spend years never making any progress or maturing because of fear. In contrast, faith uses the slightest hope to make the largest leaps forward. Faith can take the place of fear when we trust God completely.

    I don't think it's a coincidence that they built an idol that looked like the symbol of an Egyptian god. They were looking for safety and comfort in what was familiar. It's probably the same reason they longed for Egyptian food and always reminisced about Egypt as if it wasn't a place of bondage. They knew fear, but in Egypt, they knew the boundaries of its terror, the rules of their oppressors, and how to lessen their pain. Clinging to what is familiar feels safer than holding on to what is new. There's always the fear that new danger will completely destroy us. Fear can cause us to want to return to habits, places, and people that held the slightest sense of safety while we were fearful. But God doesn't want us overwhelmed by fear or holding on to old comforts to feel safe. Those old comforts may have no room in our new blessings.

I cannot promise that things will never go wrong. Rather I hope feeling safe is more about destroying the "always," the "no one, and the "never." God wants to destroy the belief that we are always defenseless, that no one is trustworthy, and that we'll never know anything different. I hope it's more about an idea of safety that strengthens our belief in ourselves and God. Troubles come, but we don't have to lose ourselves to them. 2 Corinthians 4:8-10 is evidence that in danger and confusion, there is still hope.

> **2 Corinthians 4:8-10 (NKJV)**
> 8 We are troubled on every side, yet not distressed; we are perplexed, but not in despair; 9 Persecuted, but not forsaken; cast down, but not destroyed; 10 Always bearing about in the body the dying of the Lord Jesus, that the life also of Jesus might be made manifest in our body.

Safety is knowing that what is truly important is protected by God. Our values, righteousness, and peace can emerge on the other side. The armor of God protects our salvation, peace, truth, ability to live righteously, and our faith. The essence of who we are in the Spirit is what God can protect through sickness, conflict, and heartache.

Safety

danger is an old friend
it's the space between bodies,
the bracing of my back,
the clenching of my first,
the hypervigilance,
it's the glancing of my eyes

but refuge is new to me,
breaking down walls,
laying down arms,
the ability to stand in storms
and just enjoy the rain,
can strength that's born in pain
be maintained in peace,
when i release fear
will i still find me?

Pray:

God, thank you for hiding me and protecting me. I pray fear does not rule my life decisions. Help me to operate out of the love, power, and sound mind that You've blessed me with. In areas where you have called me out of hiding, let me move boldly. Help me to identify the idols of safety I have built in my life and tear them down. Don't let fear ruin my opportunities to live in relationship and to depend on others. Increase my faith and trust in you. In Jesus name, Amen.

Reflect:

Name a place where you feel safe?
What makes you feel safe?
Have you lost opportunities because of fear?
Are there areas in your life where you can't release control?
Do you feel you have a tendency to stay hidden too long or to jump out too fast?
What areas and/or relationships could you work on taking risks in?
What has your experience taught you about safety?
What are ways we can reclaim our power?
What are indicators of danger?

Chapter 6 - Sharing

Luke 8:47 (NIV)
47 Then the woman, seeing that she could not go unnoticed, came trembling and fell at his feet. In the presence of all the people, she told why she had touched him and how she had been instantly healed.

Scriptures:

- ☐ Mark 14:32-36
- ☐ John 2:19-20
- ☐ Matthew 16:15-22
- ☐ Matthew 20:22-23
- ☐ Galatians 5:1

Maintaining the secret of abuse keeps us alone as we journey towards healing. The silence and isolation that guard secrets always seek to take up more room and steal our self-expression. Talking about what happened is a part of the journey that invites companionship. Road trips are more bearable with friends. Even if they can't help drive, their presence can help press through tiredness and long roads. At Jesus' most challenging moment, He ensured His disciples were nearby. He brought them to the Garden of Gethsemane to pray. He didn't need them to take His place or change the situation. He just wanted them there.

> **Mark 14:32 -36 (NKJV)**
> 32 Then they came to a place which was named Gethsemane; and He said to His disciples, "Sit here while I pray." 33 And He took Peter, James, and John with Him, and He began to be troubled and deeply distressed. 34 Then He said to them, "My soul is exceedingly sorrowful, even to death. Stay here and watch." 35 He went a little farther, and fell on the ground, and prayed that if it were possible, the hour might pass from Him. 36 And He said, "Abba, Father, all things are possible for You. Take this cup away from Me; nevertheless, not what I will, but what You will."

One of the most relatable moments of Jesus is when He's praying in the Garden of Gethsemane, asking God "to take this cup away from me," meaning He didn't want to die by crucifixion. I don't blame Him. The cross was a violent and cruel form of death. So I understood the why but I have always wondered about the when? How long had Jesus felt this way? How long had the thought of death been troubling His spirit? Did this apprehension happen as He entered Jerusalem, or had He been secretly walking around with it the whole time? Throughout the gospels, Jesus was slowly revealing the plan of His death and resurrection like a secret tired of being kept. It was a delicate matter disappointing the disciples' expectation of why He came. Jesus was teaching them to trust a different plan. They expected a king who was coming to live and reign forever on earth, but Jesus had come to die. He had to reveal the truth in a way that helped the disciples wrap their heads and hearts around His death and resurrection. Who knew that, at the same time, Christ was still working to accept it himself?

Secret keeping is something I know all too well. There was a time when I thought I would never tell anyone about the abuse. But part of the healing journey was learning about the time, place, and people to share with. I know what it is only to share pieces of my story, to try to say it in coded language, hoping someone will decipher it, or to say it for others' sake. I also know the beneficial difference it makes to finally reveal it all, its truth, and its effects.

Finding the courage to share isn't always easy. We question if we'll be treated differently or made to feel ashamed. There are so many statistics, and people can assume they know our issues before we voice them. Their assumptions only work to keep both women and men silent on the subject of abuse. But the more we share, the more we fight the stigmas, and the more we become people who can hear each other's stories safely and non-judgmentally. I struggled with wondering if I would be taken seriously or believed. At times, I wasn't sure that it was worth sharing. I worried I was making a big deal out of nothing. It doesn't help when we have negative experiences that seem to validate our silence. I wrote "that's why" about a negative experience at church that made me not want to tell anyone.

that's why

during sunday school
i remember their comments
people who are abused
are loose, lack intimacy skills,
promiscuous,
nontrusting,
homosexual,
frame work for the
angry black woman

and i remember seeing
those words soar
through the air
and hit the mark of my lips
like leaves cover a ditch
meant to a trap

still empty
still waiting
but no one knows
there's anything to be filled

and i remember thinking
that's why i can't tell them

can't tell them that,
growing up,
there was nothing private
on my body

if i tell them
i can't go dateless
or love another woman
without intrusive questions
or curious glances

i can't be silent
just because i'm deep
and can't weep
just for today's trouble

can't erase those lines
from my biography
can't get pass people
assuming normality
is victory in my life

can't guard my heart
with a door
without the assumption
of impenetrable walls

so i don't tell them
but my silence is still screaming

It took me a minute to get past that experience. The life of Jesus taught me lessons about sharing that helped me find the value in talking about my trauma. The first lesson is that we only have to share what we're comfortable sharing and not until we're ready. Ultimately, it's our life. We can share as much or as little as needed. Jesus exemplified this truth. Jesus had a way of sharing without really sharing. His death was described as the destruction of a temple, the drinking of a cup (Matthew 20:22), or being lifted up (John 12:32). He communicated through metaphors, stories, and questions. He often gave specific details instead of the entire picture. One example is after He cleanses the temple.

> **John 2:19-20 (NKJV)**
> 19 Jesus answered and said to them, "Destroy this temple, and in three days I will raise it up." 20 Then the Jews said, "It has taken forty-six years to build this temple, and will You raise it up in three days?"21 But He was speaking of the temple of His body. 22 Therefore, when He had risen from the dead, His disciples remembered that He had said this to them; and they believed the Scripture and the word which Jesus had said.

No one understood Jesus was talking about His own death and resurrection. He didn't want to say everything plainly and didn't intend for everyone to understand. He just needed it out in the open. There's strength in this too. This type of sharing gives us the space to pace our sharing with what our emotions and mind can handle at the time. Whatever we choose to share, it's all just a starting place needed to show us that we can handle talking about hard things.

The first time I spoke about being abused wasn't the greatest experience. I had a friend who had also been sexually abused. I hadn't told her my secret. She confided in me about her issues and felt obliged to do the same. I learned my mind wouldn't come crashing down if I said it out loud. I'd survive the words and the knowledge that someone else knew, whether they cared or not. I was strong enough to speak it. But it also made me realize that maybe it was time to tell someone who could help.

Jesus didn't start plainly revealing His death and resurrection plan until the disciples acknowledged Him as the Messiah. We should share with those who value us and our safety. Part of valuing others is being open to learning about their struggles, even when it forces us to deal with painful truths. The disciples couldn't imagine their Savior would be susceptible to death or that He would die like a criminal. Peter even told Jesus to stop saying it.

Matthew 16:15-16, 20-22 (NKJV)
15 Then he asked them, "But who do you say I am?" 16 Simon Peter answered, "You are the Messiah, the Son of the living God." 20 Then He commanded His disciples that they should tell no one that He was Jesus the Christ. 21 From that time Jesus began to show to His disciples that He must go to Jerusalem, and suffer many things from the elders and chief priests and scribes, and be killed, and be raised the third day. 22 Then Peter took Him aside and began to rebuke Him, saying, "Far be it from You, Lord; this shall not happen to You!"

They didn't want death for the savior that they loved. It is helpful to tell people who don't feel the need to pretend everything is okay. No one likes the possibility that their loved ones have been abused. No one wants to believe it's happened in their community or family. Sometimes not wanting something to happen is enough to make people not acknowledge it.

What if Jesus wanted to use that moment to tell the disciples about His feelings of distress, but because they pushed so hard against the idea of His death, Jesus kept His emotions to himself? Sometimes we confess our trauma to get a temperature check of how people will respond before sharing the effects. We may determine that they can't handle everything just yet. In these cases, Jesus shows the value of maintaining the relationship as people come to terms with the truth. When I did tell some family members, some were obviously hurt. I saw their tears and pain at what happened to me and realized that they had to go through their own healing journey. But I've been thankful for how it's brought openness to our relationship over the years.

  Another reason Jesus began to reveal the crucifixion was that some of the disciples would later die for their beliefs too. Both James and Peter would be martyred. He warned them, saying," You will indeed drink from my bitter cup" (Matthew 20:23). Sharing helps us know that we are not alone in our experience. At times, I have shared because someone told me about their experience. Although I didn't need affirmation then, I realized they did. Opening up didn't require me to be whole because I wasn't promising healing. I was just letting them know that we were surviving it together. I have talked about my experience on several occasions through poetry and ministry assignments. Whenever I share, someone in the room tells me they've been through the same thing. I've had women, men, and teenagers all come to tell me their stories. There's comfort in knowing that we're not the only ones.

We can move beyond just surviving with time and help. Eventually, Jesus would reach the Garden of Gethsemane. In the garden, Jesus was able to say everything He wanted. He said it plainly and to someone who could help, His Father. God sent an angel to strengthen Jesus. I don't know if the cross would have happened without that moment. We all need the space to admit when life's struggles and pressure have become too much.

In the garden, the disciples were weren't actively present. The weight of their grief caused them to continually fall asleep. They may have been asleep but at least they had accepted the truth. Jesus did try to wake them up and that's what inspired the poem "Awake". I think when we talk about our abuse, we are working to wake people up, if not for ourselves, then for others who may benefit or be protected. They may be awakened in a way that affects the issue of abuse in families and communities.

Awake

all He would ask
was that they stay awake,
in a garden, Jesus' sweat
became like drops of blood,
in some dark space
and somewhere else,
in times gone and come,
a child waiting for someone
to stay awake,
bleeds and sweats and prays
for the strength of angels,
for the attention of those
who promised to stay alert
to watch and guard
when they and salvation
are only a stone's throw away,
only one room down,
only one person removed

and that child waits like Christ
knowing that someone
fell asleep,
couldn't stay awake
and someone's temptation
has shaken the faith and
the body of a child

and just like Jesus on the cross,
something inside dies,
and i have died that death,
children everyday die this death
waiting for someone
to hear our screams,
to believe our whispers,
to write our stories,
save our dreams,

and resurrect our innocence

waiting for someone to wake up
and know that their
presence, not their hope
will make a difference

There's power in being able to discuss our experiences with someone who is trustworthy and equipped to help. A few years ago, I was driving to work when I got a message that a counselor I knew had passed away. I hadn't spoken to her in almost 15 years, but the news was so heartbreaking that I cried all the way to work. I remember being in her office, telling her about my past, and talking about my feelings. I remember her attentiveness, kindness, and compassion. There's so much heaviness concealed in the silence we carry. But talking to her lifted a weight and gave me hope that I wouldn't always feel so lost.

In counseling, she had a way of getting me to see how trauma had affected my life in ways I wasn't fully acknowledging. She was patient with how and when I revealed everything that happened and seemed to always know when there was more truth to be told. I was able to talk about the insecurities, fear, and shame in a safe place. Because she was also a Christian, we could talk about how my faith could inform my healing process. The time with her brought healing and helped me find myself growing closer to God. After we heal, our sharing can become a testimony.

When Jesus resurrected from the dead, His experience became the gospel, the good news we are to spread to everyone. It became a testimony of power, love, and sacrifice. Jesus understands the power of testifying after we've been healed. He encourages glorifying God by sharing how He has healed us. He offered the woman with the issue of blood a chance to share her story of healing. While Jesus was in a crowd, she knelt and touched his garment which healed her issue (Luke 8:43-48). She planned to go away quietly but Jesus stopped the crowd and offered her the opportunity to share. She could have taken her healing, ran off and said nothing. I'm glad she decided to share.

> **Luke 8:47 (NIV)**
> 47 Then the woman, seeing that she could not go unnoticed, came trembling and fell at his feet. In the presence of all the people, she told why she had touched him and how she had been instantly healed.

Her story, to this day, serves as a testimony of God's ability to heal. I pray that for us, that our life is so dramatically shifted for the better, that the change can't go unnoticed. That we'll have to answer for our peace, joy, and courage because it is so tangible, but unexpected. There are some of us who are called to share. Being chosen by God is being chosen to live our life out loud. It is a recognition that even our stories and our secrets are on the altar to use if God should choose. Our stories aren't something we silence; they are what we steward for God's glory. Scripture lets us know that the "the testimony of Jesus is the spirit of prophecy." (Revelation 19:10, NKJV) If we can see the movement of Jesus in our lives from the suffering to the healing, then our witness becomes prophetic to others. We can speak a future to someone who has given up on tomorrow.

But healing isn't based on testifying. We don't have to rush to it. I have a tendency to rush to wanting to help people overcome what they're going through by sharing my own experiences. I see a lesson in everything. It's a strength of mine, it makes me a good preacher and teacher. But honestly, it also makes me tend to rush the recovery process, focus on others to the point of self-neglect, and lean towards excusing my suffering because it helps. There is something in me that is unsatisfied with the idea that tragedy just happens but that is a part of living in a world of free will.

I think the belief that God causes suffering only to help others is bad theology. Just because God uses a situation doesn't mean that He caused it. The wrong belief will cause us to live as if the cost of healing is service or the evidence of healing is being used to help others. Maybe that's why so many people hurry to help before they're fully recovered. We want their pain validated; we need to believe that it wasn't for nothing. Free yourself from the weight of that burden. I'm learning more and more that the "why" isn't as important as the "what's next". Yes, God can use it for good but even in the places that He doesn't, I'm just thankful that He wants us to be healed.

God heals me because God loves me. There's a scripture that says, "It is for freedom we have been set free" (Galatians 5:1). That's pretty amazing. It doesn't say we've been set free to help others, to free others, to serve, or to be used. We have been set free because God values freedom. In the same way, we have been healed because God values healing. He loves us enough to want us whole. So if we never write a book, or tell our story before a crowd, God's power is still leading to restoration and abundance. We owe no debt to freedom. I want us to take the time to heal. Go through the process and be healed because it's the best thing for us. It is for wholeness we have been healed. The rest is just icing on the cake.

Pray:

Dear God, help me to get my voice back in every area of my life. Show me who to share with. Give me the how and the when to share with people who have your heart and will walk along this journey with me. Allow my sharing to bring healing for me. If you call me to share it as a testimony, may it glorify you and point others to your throne. In the name of Jesus, Amen.

Reflect:

Who do you want to share your story with?
If you have never told anyone, what's stopping you?
If you have shared, what was great about others responses and what troubled you?
What effects have carrying a secret had on your life, on your relationships, on your ability to be authentic in every situation?
What cultural/family values make silence acceptable/preferred?

Chapter 7 - Feelings

Psalm 143:1-4 (AMP)
1 Hear my prayer, O Lord, Listen to my supplications! Answer me in Your faithfulness and in Your righteousness. 2 And do not enter into judgment with Your servant, For in Your sight no man living is righteous or justified. 3 For the enemy has persecuted me, He has crushed my life down to the ground; He has made me dwell in dark places, like those who have been long dead. 4 Therefore my spirit is overwhelmed and weak within me [wrapped in darkness]:
My heart grows numb within me.

Scriptures:

- ☐ Psalm 62:2
- ☐ Psalm 137
- ☐ Psalm 143:1-4
- ☐ Ezekiel 3:8
- ☐ Ephesians 2:19-21
- ☐ Exodus 17:1-7
- ☐ Psalm 126:5

A hardened heart is a counterfeit for wholeness. But it's a counterfeit that can easily convince those whose pain is deep or long-lasting. We do what we have to in order to survive. It's not always about whether we'll die but whether our hearts and minds can survive the trauma intact. Our body knows danger, so it braces itself; our mind knows danger, so it shatters its memory. When our emotions experience overwhelming danger, the heart hardens until we become numb to everything. If we try hard enough, we can convince ourselves that healing is the absence of emotions, and that numbness is not only necessary to live but is advantageous in the long run. It makes all the emotional sense in the world.

At least, it initially made sense to me. Consider all the images of stones and rocks used throughout scripture. Jesus, himself, is the cornerstone (Ephesians 2:20), and God is our rock and salvation (Psalm 62:2). When God doesn't want Ezekiel to be afraid, He promises to make his face hard as stone (Ezekiel 3:8). Stone symbolizes strength, impenetrability, and the ability to carry a heavy load. Stone is supposed to survive. Castles are built of stone, and monuments that have lasted centuries are built of stone. It is as if when we want something with minimal risk of destruction, stone would be a wise choice, and God seems to agree in every area except one: our heart.

We learn what God intends for our hearts in the book of Ezekiel. It almost seems unfair that God, who highlights the benefits of stone, tells Ezekiel that He intends to replace the people's heart of stone with a heart of flesh.

> **Ezekiel 36:24-28**
> 24 For I will take you from among the nations, gather you out of all countries, and bring you into your own land. 25 Then I will sprinkle clean water on you, and you shall be clean; I will cleanse you from all your filthiness and from all your idols. 26 I will give you a new heart and put a new spirit within you; I will take the heart of stone out of your flesh and give you a heart of flesh. 27 I will put My Spirit within you and cause you to walk in My statutes, and you will keep My judgments and do them. 28 Then you shall dwell in the land that I gave to your fathers; you shall be My people, and I will be your God.

If the people were using a heart of stone to survive the pain of exile, wouldn't a heart of flesh be counterproductive? The flesh is soft, vulnerable, and easily hurt. It's affected by what's happening around us, for better or worse. Is it fair to ask people to let down their guard, sometimes the only guard they can truly control? I wonder if Ezekiel wondered how beneficial it would be for the Israelites. They had been in exile for years. They were torn from their land, their families, and their temple, which felt as if God had rejected them. Their captors mocked their faith, and they didn't know if they would be able to return home or would they be forced to make this strange place their home. Is it any wonder their hearts became like stone.

The hardening doesn't happen overnight. But the longer they remained in exile, the harder their emotions became to deal with. Psalm 137 describes their experience of exile.

> **Psalm 137:1-3 (NASB)**
> 1 By the rivers of Babylon,
> There we sat down and wept,
> When we remembered Zion.
> 2 Upon the willows in the midst of it
> We hung our harps.
> 3 For there our captors demanded of us songs,
> And our tormentors, jubilation, saying,
> "Sing for us one of the songs of Zion!"

They wept when they remembered their home. They hung up their instruments of praise and worship. Then their enemies forced them to sing, to perform songs that were reflective of a peace and safety that no longer belonged to them. This process of hardening involves grief at losing what you think you can never get back, whether that's joy, a person, or a way of life. Then at some point we stop our praise, we stop our worship. We can't find the sincerity for them anymore. On top of that, life's expectations and routines force us to keep doing the same things we no longer want. So even though we don't feel it, and don't want it, we are forced to perform. We are forced to get through every day and our hearts hardened so we can carry the weight of the performance. Our hearts are hardened to prove to our enemies that they haven't gotten the best of us. The hardening of my heart was an unintentional process for me too. I didn't just decide to stop feeling. I felt that crying made me look weak which made me vulnerable. I just kept pushing that emotion down, kept telling myself not to, until I didn't have to say it anymore. It just became the automatic response. And all my other emotions followed the lead.

    I'm grateful that God understands our emotions. God understands why hearts harden and is compassionate towards us. God doesn't say that He would heal their heart in exile. He waited until they were safe. He wanted them to be in a place where they could receive what they longed for. If he brought them back to their land but left their hearts the way they were, they wouldn't be able to enjoy the blessing of it. And if He gave them a heart of flesh while in exile, they may have lost the strength to love. I am thankful for God's patience and wrote the poem Kingdom to give imagery to how far I believe God goes to rescue our heart.

kingdom

the kingdom of heaven is like
the heart of a woman hidden
in stone, when God found it,
he hid it again, and in His compassion
took the life of His only begotten Son
to purchase her entire being

and all so that no one else could
lay claim to the ground
in which He found the heart
that he perfectly created
but lost behind emotions
hardened after being unused

hid it so that no one could
force it deeper into stone
by stepping on it, crushing it because
they couldn't distinguish
it from any other rock

gave up His own
so when He finally exposed
the heart, it would be
only in the power of His spirit,
the safety of His presence,
in the resting of His peace

thought it was so much to be treasured
that He bought her entire being
to make the crown worthy of its jewels,
the melody worthy of its beat
the body worthy of its heart

purchased her so he could heal
her scars, her wounds, her marks
left from those who never
found the treasure or

understood that God seeks
to be most reflected in the heart

One night, I remember praying and feeling as if God was telling me that it's okay to cry. Didn't He know that I was trying to hold everything together? Didn't he know that my logic was sound? I'd reasoned if it weren't for emotions, it would be so much easier to move on from bad events. Memories keep you attached to the past, but emotions tighten that pull with a suffocating grip until every move away requires the cooperation of our entire being. A being whose heart and head often move in opposite directions. I figured if it wasn't for emotions, some suffering wouldn't find me as if trauma feeds on tears or lingered among fear. So, feeling nothing seemed like the answer to the past and the future, like a guard against other timelines invading my present. Hurt from the past and anxiety from the future couldn't find me in the present.

I couldn't imagine going back to being open. The Israelites probably struggled to imagine it too. To go back to feeling like they could open themselves to hope, and joy and love. To go back to feeling sadness, anger and disappointment in nondestructive ways. It probably seemed almost as impossible as going home again. But that's the thing about God, He was already planning the impossible of gathering the people together and returning them home.

In my life, telling me to cry was like getting water from a stone. Naturally, it's impossible, but God already proved that nothing is impossible. In Exodus, there's a miracle in the Bible of water coming from a stone (Exodus 17:1-7). Imagine that, from a hard solid stone comes refreshing water. Only God can do something like that, to bring water out of something dry, hard, and solid. I remember crying that night and I don't know exactly how long it'd been, but it felt like I was releasing years of tears from behind a dam of stone. Like there was enough water in that stone to quench the thirst of a nation, there were enough tears to quench the longing of expression, to wash away all the dirt, the resistance, and the mistakes I made because of the numbing. I didn't know how much I needed it, and I wondered if it would always take a miracle to get there.

The miracle doesn't have to end. The ability to feel, to express and receive love, and all other emotions are a miracle in a world filled with so much pain. The Bible says that the world will know us by our love, I don't think that means they just know us because we're kind to each other, but that they'll be amazed at our love that survives pain, heartache, devastation, disappointment. Our love can keep going, keep resurrecting when others would've stopped, when others would have been scared or see no advantage. Being willing to feel it all and express it all is God working through us every single day. God meant for it to be a way of life. So, my heart had to be turned in flesh, because flesh allows it to happen consistently. Flesh is healing and restoration.

Restoration opens the door for good things to come in and negativity to leave. I don't think a hardened heart feels nothing, but that its real feelings are hidden so far beneath the surface, they can't be heard and they aren't strong enough to move any other parts of our life. They can't push us towards love or risk or joy or pain. The anger gets traps inside. The hate gets trapped inside. The fear gets trapped inside. And we need flesh so those things can flow out of us. Now emotions like joy, hope and excitement can flow inside of us.

A heart of flesh allows us to love one another. We need to be open to experiencing love wherever it comes from, family and friends. There was a point in my life that I wondered if I would ever get married. I didn't have long relationships. I wasn't sure I would stay with someone long enough to give them the chance to love me or for me to love them. I didn't' know that I ever wanted to trust anybody like that. I refused to be invested emotionally. As soon as things got too serious, I was done. When I got to the point where I did want to love, I realized I couldn't do it with a hardened heart.

It would be so much easier if we could just look at someone and know if their intentions were good or not. I knew men in my life that broke trust and men in my life that I trusted with my life, it took time to figure out which one they were. It would be so much easier if abusers looked a certain way, but we can find them as easily down a dark alley as we can in a boardroom. I had to learn it was ok to give someone a chance. That's when I wrote Eve's curse. I wanted to express the fears that came along with meeting someone and the hope that they would be different.

eve's curse

and my desire shall be for him,
him who rapes, molests and mutilates,
him whose masculinity is defined
by domination of hers,
him who has conquered
the world on the graves of hers,

him who has born his warriors,
his heroes
from hers whose face
and names are not remembered,
him who has defined strength and power
against hers labeled weak and foolish,
him who has hung witches,
burned mystics,
left hers exposed to nature,
him who has wrote her out of history
and into submission

and the curse for her is not this desire,
but that she must desire in the face
of all that he represents,
all that he has done
to her mothers,
her sisters,
and her daughters

and how can she bear this desire
in the fear that giving into it
will give permission for hims
throughout time to find their way
into her lovers eyes, his mind

fear that she will know his lust,
not his love, be taken back into memories
of abuse, misuse, incest

fear that she will be his outlet
of anger, of shame
and she will bear his fist, his hand
his screams,

bear all the fear that the world puts on him
in the surrendering of her hands,
the hanging of her head

fear that she will be placed once again
in roles that begin with house,
where tradition has said she belongs
when prophecy is propelling
her into pulpits

but her desire shall be for him
and she cannot leave
for as much as she fears,
she really does desire him,
really does long for his embrace,
longs for God to see the reflection
of His face in their combining identities

so she must work to forgive his history
that has always imposed him
on top and in front of her
and she must find a him who can repent
for history and love her into a new story

Emotions allow us to love God. They also allow us to receive God's love, to be fully convinced of His concern for us and the pleasure He takes in our presence. Love is also related to our ability to obey. Without loving God, we won't obey Him. Love is what makes us willing to obey. There's a tendency to downplay emotions in Christianity, but there is no worship without emotions. There is no sacrifice without a tender and broken heart. Without emotions there is no conviction to lead us to want to do better and please God.

> **Psalm 56:8 (TPL)**
> 8 You've kept track of all my wandering and my weeping, you've stored my many tears in your bottle - not one will be lost.

Having a heart of flesh taught me the benefits of tears. My favorite scripture in the Bible is "Those who sow in tears shall reap in joy" (Psalm 126:5). It made me feel like my tears weren't wasted. The road to healing does look like going backward and in circles at times. But, the nature of retracing our steps isn't all bad, especially if seeds were sown along the way. We go along familiar paths to find the fruit from seeds of hope, obedience and even suffering. That fruit of wisdom, strength and awareness are ours for the taking. That is the nature of sowing and reaping. It's retracing our steps and taking advantage of what time has allowed us to grow. When we take those steps with our heart and emotions, we can see evidence of that growth. When the roads towards healing lead towards the wilderness, rain can be rare, but tears will suffice. We can water the driest of earth. It's bringing water to the desert; we are walking miracles.

Pray:

God, I pray that you give me a heart of flesh. Help me to recognize where my heart has become hardened. Give me the freedom to feel every range of emotions, to receive and give love, to know that you are with me through every feeling. Help me to trust you with my joy and with my tears and to trust that they make my life worthwhile. In Jesus name, Amen.

Reflection

Are there certain emotions you have a hard time expressing?

What is your fear in expressing those emotions?

How do you deal with your feelings from abuse?

Do you seek others or turn inward when you have negative emotions?

Chapter 8 - Triggers

1 Kings 17:18
18 So she said to Elijah, "What have I to do with you, O man of God? Have you come to me to bring my sin to remembrance, and to kill my son?"

Scriptures

- 1 Kings 17:13-24
- Joshua 8:31

help

i feel the tilting of the earth
when i sway too far,
feel the crumbling
of the earth's core within
my bones if i step too hard,
i'm a pebble causing ripples
that birth storms
on shores too far to know
the level of my harm,
i'm a bullet from the past
aiming at future joy

That poem is a little dramatic, right? I know, but I'm a poet, so I have that right. And honestly, life tends to feel like this. It's as if the smallest incidents shift my world and rewrite my current reality as the ending to a life chapter I thought was closed. When we are convinced that we have beat the fear, shame, and pain of previous trauma, new disrupting experiences can bring them up again. We believe that the same fear and pain never really left but were just waiting for the right moment to attack. It's as if they came to remind us that we never really escaped them in the first place.

I think that's what the widow in 1 Kings 17 must have felt when she asked Elijah, "Did you come here to remind me of my sin?" This woman experienced the trauma of going through a famine. Things got so bad that she lost hope and decided to prepare one last meal for herself and her son before they died of starvation (1 Kings 17:12). The prophet Elijah shows up, and a miracle happens. God provides enough food to sustain them through the famine.

> **1 Kings 17:13-18 (NKJV)**
> 13 And Elijah said to her, "Do not fear; go *and* do as you have said, but make me a small cake from it first, and bring *it* to me; and afterward make *some* for yourself and your son. 14 For thus says the LORD God of Israel: 'The bin of flour shall not be used up, nor

shall the jar of oil run dry, until the day the LORD sends rain on the earth.' " **15** So she went away and did according to the word of Elijah; and she and he and her household ate for *many* days. **16** The bin of flour was not used up, nor did the jar of oil run dry, according to the word of the LORD which He spoke by Elijah. **17** Now it happened after these things *that* the son of the woman who owned the house became sick. And his sickness was so serious that there was no breath left in him. **18** So she said to Elijah, "What have I to do with you, O man of God? Have you come to me to bring my sin to remembrance, and to kill my son?"

Soon that memory of lack is gone. She is secure and hopeful, knowing that her family is safe from danger. They survived. But just as she gets comfortable, trauma hits again. Her son dies. She was facing death during the famine, and now she had to deal with death again. She couldn't separate this experience from the past one. That's when she confronts the prophet with the question, "Did you come here to remind me of my sin?" Her mind went to the worst about herself even though Elijah never mentioned her past. We can't control our initial reactions or how our memory makes connections between events. But we do have a choice on whether we choose to dwell on them. After our initial reaction, it is helpful to remind ourselves that these are two separate events in order to gain perspective.

When I was in grad school, I joined a new church. Everything was going great until one night when the pastor called. What started off as a friendly conversation ended with sexually inappropriate comments. I ended the conversation. When he reached back out, I thought it was to apologize. Instead, it was to stress how telling anyone could be damaging to him and his reputation. As far as I thought I'd come, I felt like that little girl caught off guard by an unpredictable man again. I felt ashamed, objectified, and burdened with another secret. I struggled not to connect that situation to my past abuse. But it reminded me of everything I was trying to get away from. The questions afterward were worse than the experience. Is this what happens when I trust? Can I ever let down my guard? Was I right all along that I was weak? I needed to take some time to really reflect.

Once I was able to step back emotionally and separate the events, I could handle it with greater composure. It allowed me to deal with it for what it was. I was able to remind myself that I was safe and not a little girl. I had the option to figure out what was next and to walk away. When we stay focused on what's happening now, we can turn our attention to what's needed for healing this situation. We can look for God in the situation. If the widow had taken time to find God in her situation, maybe she would have realized that she was literally living in a miracle. The same God who caused her jar to never empty was strong enough to deal with death. Maybe it would have changed her question from "Did you come to remind me of my sin" to "What will God do now?"

I'm sure it wasn't just the similarity of the experience that affected the widow but also the similarity in emotions. She was preparing to die when Elijah met her, so she already knew grief. She had already mourned her family's loss. And if she had no one to turn to, it meant that she had already likely lost people to death. The grief of the famine, the grief of her son's death and the regret from her sin collided in greater heartache. The woman added to her grief by adding in all the feelings she had about her previous sin. Any feelings of regret or condemnation came rushing back.

Even if the experience is different, similar emotions can trigger past anxiety. I remember being rushed into emergency surgery because of an ectopic pregnancy for the 2nd time in less than a year. After recovering physically, I had to heal emotionally from those losses. It wasn't just grief, but also feeling helpless as if I had no power over my body. Nothing prepared me for how similar emotions of helplessness and heartache would send my thoughts back to being abused. Memories I hadn't thought of in years invaded my everyday thoughts. And the weight of carrying both experiences made me want to give up on everything. I had to turn to God.

God eventually showed me there was still a level of healing I needed from the past. The present exposed a vulnerability I had just learned to live with. Healing has layers to it and it's easy to accept that some issues will always be there. It's easy to ignore them because we've managed to progress without addressing the issues. We've compensated so well that we've forgotten they were there. But new trauma will make a gaping hole of the smallest crack in our healing. I had dealt with the anger and the offense, but after going to counseling, I realized that I still had issues of regret. Thoughts of what I could have done differently while pregnant and while being abused plagued my mind. I couldn't do anything about either situation now, but coming to peace with what I couldn't change healed my present and my past.

too much

what does this look like
after losing pregnancies,
that nagging thought that
maybe i wasn't completely forgiven
for the past, that grace paid a part
but left a debt that peace had to pay
and fear was waiting to collect,
what was a whisper during the first loss
became a scream after the second
as it dug up wounds
whose scabs had convinced me
they were healed.
brought up thoughts of
if only i hadn't offended,
broken that law,
let this happen,
been slower, instead of faster
if only i'd lived a life of innocence,
it looks like condemnation
for what was already forgiven
and the need for God to remind
that we don't have to
remember our past mistakes,
our futures can escape yesterday
and that God's grace
has already paved the way

The widow found the healing she was seeking. When she questioned Elijah, he prayed to God until her son was healed. God's power was still working for her. God's power is still working for us.

1 Kings 17

> 20 Then he cried out to the LORD and said, "O LORD my God, have You also brought tragedy on the widow with whom I lodge, by killing her son?" 21 And he stretched himself out on the child three times, and cried out to the LORD and said, "O LORD my God, I pray, let this child's soul come back to him." 22 Then the LORD heard the voice of Elijah; and the soul of the child came back to him, and he revived. 23 And Elijah took the child and brought him down from the upper room into the house, and gave him to his mother. And Elijah said, "See, your son lives!" 24 Then the woman said to Elijah, "Now by this I know that you *are* a man of God, *and* that the word of the LORD in your mouth *is* the truth."

Just like God got us through past obstacles, His power remains to get us through current and future ones. Healing took time and patience. God wants us to be completely healed and to have peace. The Bible uses the word shalom to describe peace. Shalom means wholeness or completion. It can refer to a stone without cracks (Joshua 8:31). It means that all parts of our lives are whole, and that all parts of our complex being has been restored to unity.

God wants this type of peace for us, but it means dealing with every place of unrest, no matter how small. Until we get there, though, we have to offer ourselves grace as we struggle with current distress. Be gentle with ourselves when we're not reacting as we think we should. The Prince of Peace, the Prince of Shalom is doing the work of shalom and restoring us to wholeness.

Pray:

May my losses not be compounded
with unrelated guilt.
may my shame find
a grave so deep
that resurrection can't uplift,
may every failure
feel like the one and only,
may I forgive myself,
completely and unshakably
even in the face of memory,
may I start each day
welcoming the new mercy
and may condemnation
find no room in me,
I am occupied by grace.
Amen.

Reflect:

What triggers do you have?

What do your triggers teach you about your healing journey?

Chapter 9 – Forgiveness

Ephesians 4:31-32
31 Get rid of all bitterness, rage and anger, brawling and slander, along with every form of malice. 32 Be kind and compassionate to one another, forgiving each other, just as in Christ God forgave you.

Scriptures

- ☐ Jonah 4
- ☐ Ephesians 4 :26-32
- ☐ Matthew 6:14-15
- ☐ Luke 17:3-4
- ☐ Luke 23:33-34

I couldn't take it back once I put the letter in the post office mailbox. What was I thinking? I panicked and wanted for a minute to figure out time travel or harass an employee to get my letter back. So many questions came to mind about the letter I just mailed. It was a letter expressing how I felt and offering forgiveness to the man who abused me. Was I being stupid? He had never acknowledged what he'd done to me. Would he even respond? Would he deny it? Would everyone find out about it? So many questions I hadn't entirely made peace with, but I still knew this was the right thing to do for me. Something I had already done within me but now wanted to express. I hadn't come to this decision easily. I can't imagine that anyone does, but it provided some closure for that experience that allowed me to walk away with my heart.

My heart's emotions have always felt complicated. Most of the time, when asked how I'm feeling, I respond with either good or bad. It's not a brush-off but often a sincere struggle to name the specific emotions ebbing and flowing beneath the surface. Rarely, in the present moment, am I able to name the pieces that make up the entirety of my mood. I need space and time to reflect. A "bad" that's made up of depression and isolation is very different from a "bad" that's made up of rejection and anger. A "good" that's made up of excitement differs from a "good" that's made up of hope. The response is different. All I knew was that I was angry. And anger was shifting and changing me into a person I didn't want to become. Anger was inviting resentment and restlessness. I had to seek God for the correct response because I wanted peace. God showed me that forgiveness was the answer.

unforgiveness

unforgiveness rots the soul.
the last time i felt whole
was depression, anger, hate, no..
7 emotions ago,
the last time i cried was 3.
one meal for every 5 horizons
to prove i can control something
if not my pain.
I can't sleep for remembering
the abuse, the fear, the words that echo
"nobody loves you,"
this whisper in my ear "forgive him"
but if I couldn't stop him
maybe I can't control this

now my heart has grown hard
like cracked glass about to shatter,
my shoulders drop further,
my head hangs lower,
my frown begins to crease
permanent wrinkles in my youth,
i vow to never tell another man i love you,
and i can't even raise my hands to praise
the God i serve because my bitterness
extends to my fingertips
and more reserves of tragedy
than triumph overflow
from my soul to my lips,
and behind my hallelujahs are echoes of
"i'm hurting and i'm angry"
that only God can hear

then there's this gap between
true love's definition
and my imitation of smiles, of living,
my mimicking of wrapping my arms
around another human being
and giving of myself
that i'm too occupied defending
to ever let God fill,
and i hate myself for holding on this long
when chances are my violator
never wonders if i've considered suicide
or if i sleep at night
but today I choose to forgive
because i'm tired of the fight,
i forgive him because if to hate a man
in your heart is to kill him,
i've murdered him a thousand times
so now I need God's forgiveness,
I forgive him because
tomorrow the sun will shine
and I might not be here to see it
and just besides seeming
small in comparison
hating him will no earthly consequence
but a partial soul never finds rest
not even in eternity,
and I forgive him because
one day a man will fall in love
with my poetry and I want all of me
to love him back,
but most importantly I forgive
because finally the call of destiny
is louder than that unspoken memory
and i am determined to live free

Most people are suspicious of forgiveness. We've seen too many people taken advantage of after offering it. We've tried forgiveness before while doubting if we ever truly accomplished it. We can begin to wonder what good it does. But I figured if I had faith in God, I should trust him too. For me, the book of Jonah has always been about the difference between faith and trust in God. We can believe that God exists and that He's powerful, loving, and compassionate, while not trusting that He's making the best decision for our lives. Jonah had faith that God was gracious and forgiving. He simply didn't trust that God was doing the right thing with those attributes. It all started with an assignment that God gave Jonah.

Jonah 1:1-2
1 The word of the Lord came to Jonah the son of Amittai, saying, 2 "Arise, go to Nineveh, the great city, and cry out against it, because their wickedness has come up before Me.

Jonah was angry at the nation who had abused his people. Jonah was an Israelite sent to Nineveh, the capital city of the Assyrian empire. The Assyrians were Israel's enemies because they continually attacked and brutalized the Israelites. Jonah was so angry that he refused to give them God's message. He knew that God was prepared to destroy them but that their repentance could change God's mind. And with all the death and torment caused by the Assyrians, it was probably easy to think they deserved all the destruction coming their way.

Jonah never said he was angry with them, but his actions showed his heart. Forgiveness can't truly happen where we are unwilling to acknowledge those feelings. There were times where I couldn't admit my anger, but it was showing up in life. I didn't want to admit it because anger felt wrong. But not admitting it doesn't make it less true. It also felt hard to recognize because my anger doesn't always look like rage. It isn't loud or aggressive. Sometimes, it's quiet and brooding or complaining and avoidant. My emotions made me feel guilty and out of control. But God's message showed me that anger is a normal response to wickedness. Anger isn't a sin. It's okay to realize that we're hurting or offended.

I wasn't alone in my anger. Jonah's story let me know that God is angry when abuse happens. God is not indifferent to our experiences. He is moved by our anger. Throughout scripture, God hears the cry of a group or individual and responds. When He heard the blood of Abel cry, He came and punished Cain for killing him.

When He heard the Israelites cry out against their Egyptian slave masters, He came and delivered them. Our anger and hurting can set God's justice into motion. He takes on our anger so we can let it go.

The process of letting anger go is forgiveness. God asks us to forgive because He knows the danger of holding on to anger. God says, "Don't let the sun go down on your anger" (Ephesians 4:26). Anger that lasts too long begins to continually need the input of rehearsing hurt. It takes mental and emotional capacity that could go to better use. Replaying memories and reliving emotions feed into anger. We are meditating on negativity, and whatever we meditate on will grow and flourish within us. When we remain resentful, anger becomes a raging fire fueled by our thoughts.

The longer we refuse to forgive, the more the initial hurts turn towards bitterness and malice. We eventually become so bitter that the source of our anger becomes harder to extinguish. And because we stay hurt, everything in our life suffers for it. Moments of joy compete with hateful emotions. Ephesians 4:31-32 lets us know some of the feelings that unforgiveness can conceal.

Ephesians 4:31-32
31 Get rid of all bitterness, rage and anger, brawling and slander, along with every form of malice. 32 Be kind and compassionate to one another, forgiving each other, just as in God forgave you.

Jonah received the message and found the quickest boat heading in the opposite direction. That's the danger of unforgiveness. It will cause us to go in the opposite direction of God to maintain it. It will cause us to do things out of character. Unforgiveness grows in its ability to make us feel negatively and act sinfully in response to our anger. God warns that anger shouldn't lead us to sin (Ephesians 4:26). We know our anger has gone too far and lasted too long when it's causing us to be outside of God's will. We don't always understand the effects on our relationship with God when we refuse Him. Sometimes, we think saying no to a request or desire of God is not a big deal but in Jonah, it's literally described as fleeing from the presence of God (Jonah 1:3). When Jonah sinned and turned from God's presence, he was put in the belly of a whale where he prayed and agreed to make it right with God.

Jonah 2:9 (NKJV)
9 But I will sacrifice to You With the voice of thanksgiving; I will pay what I have vowed. Salvation *is* of the LORD."

Part of forgiveness's power is positioning ourselves to receive God's forgiveness. Giving forgiveness shows the necessary humility to receive forgiveness and the power to change. In Matthew 6, God places the condition of forgiveness on our ability to forgive.

Matthew 6
14 For if you forgive other people for their offenses, your heavenly Father will also forgive you. 15 But if you do not forgive other people, then your Father will not forgive your offenses.

Forgiving is a recognition that we have all sinned and are all in need of God's mercy. I would love to say that dealing with trauma never caused me to sin, but that wouldn't be true. I want to think that if I hadn't been abused, I would never have sinned, but that would be a lie, too. I've done stupid and shameful things. I have sinned knowing I was absolutely wrong at the time and sinned in ways I would later come to realize were wrong. I know that I am in need of God's forgiveness and while we may compare sins, God does not. The "at least I'm not doing that" excuse won't change the consequences of an unrepented life.

To repent means to turn away from the sin we are committing. Forgiveness is not an invitation to allow harm to continue in our lives. Look at what God's forgiveness offered the people of Nineveh - change or be overturned.

Jonah 3
4 Then Jonah began to go through the city one day's walk; and he cried out and said, "Forty more days, and Nineveh will be overthrown." 5 Then the people of Nineveh believed in God; and they called a fast and put on sackcloth, from the greatest to the least of them.

Jonah may have had a genuine concern for his nation that Nineveh would return to their wicked ways. Forgiveness can feel scary. It can feel as if it compromises safety. Our forgiveness can offer the same change or boundaries requirement to create a safe place for us. Unlike God, we can't always trust repentance because we can't see people's hearts, so safety has a place in forgiveness. Forgiveness doesn't mean that we must forfeit justice. We can expose and forgive. We can press charges and forgive. Forgiveness doesn't mean we have to stay in the position to get hurt again to prove I've really forgiven. God forgives, but He also separates the harmful to defend the weak.

After Jonah obeyed God, he lingered near the city. He stayed close enough to the Assyrians to see how they would respond. Will they apologize? Will they repent? He offered God's forgiveness, not his own. He probably figured their repentance was more about fearing God than apologizing for what they had done. And his unforgiveness, like ours, will keep us tied to the situation listening. It will keep us linked to our offender's life when we can entirely let them go. Jonah was willing to sit there and be miserable rather than move on. We need to forgive to move on to our next assignment.

Jonah stays long enough to see the people repent and he complains to God about choosing to withholding destruction. God tries to explain by asking Jonah a question.

> **Jonah 4:11**
> And should not I spare Nineveh, that great city, wherein are more than sixscore thousand persons that cannot discern between their right hand and their left hand; and also much cattle?

I love that God doesn't leave us with an answer. Jonah had to figure it out for himself and so do we. Part of moving forward is having peace with how God chooses to deal with our offender. Jonah wasn't at peace with God's compassion for his enemy. We can't forgive if we are conflicted with God's forgiveness. Are we reconciled to the fact that God can forgive our abusers? Are we like

Jonah, or do we want God reconciled to His creation? And maybe no one will understand this if they don't believe in an eternal heaven and hell, but I don't want anybody with my name over their head in hell. God doesn't want any to perish. Do we love God enough to want Him to have all that He wants?

I believe Jonah's answer to God's question was essential to his own well-being. God could have chosen anybody for this assignment. Why did he choose the man who obviously hated the Assyrians? Jonah's assignment may have been for him as much as it was for the Assyrians. God wanted to teach Jonah about compassion and concern. He invited Jonah into conversation to persuade him. God wanted to get him to understand His love for all creation. And God wanted him to be more than obedient, He wanted Jonah to feel that compassion for himself.

I had to get to the point where forgiveness was for me and no one else. I didn't want to do just because it was the Christian thing to do, although that honestly should be enough. I also didn't want to do it because that's the answer to abuse that many ministers give as the first and only way of healing. If healing is a journey, the land of forgiveness is where preachers will take you, come to a rolling stop long enough for you to exit the car, and wave while they speed off. It's the first and the most straightforward answer. People tell us that if we'd just forgive, we could move on. But it can't be the only step in healing because it doesn't heal all.

And if you're like me, it couldn't be my first step in healing. I couldn't do it quickly. It's hard to offer forgiveness if we are still struggling with who to blame. Feeling rushed to forgive can make us feel like failures. I struggled to forgive a story still coming together in my mind. There were definite steps of acknowledgement and truth that I needed before I could completely forgive. Healing starts before forgiveness but cannot be finished without forgiveness.

I know everyone won't understand forgiveness. It's easy for others to mock or view it as a weakness. Obeying God's won't always make us feel good and won't always be popular. Forgiveness is a spiritual act that takes the power of God. The fact that we have been abused suggests that at some moment in our lives, control was taken from us, and it's easy to believe that we can never gain control again. For me, forgiveness is a form of power. It means making a choice that no one can make for me. It takes strength. And it takes greater strength if no one has apologized.

One of the first questions we often ask is do we have to forgive if our offender never asks for forgiveness. Scriptures that talk about forgiveness often have an "if" attached.

Luke 17:3-4
3 So watch yourselves. If your brother or sister sins against you, rebuke them; and if they repent, forgive them. 4 Even if they sin against you seven times in a day and seven times come back to you saying 'I repent,' you must forgive them."

Scriptures like these seem to let us off the hook if a person doesn't repent. The truth is God often makes concessions for the frailty of our hearts. He will allow things He doesn't want for us. One example is that God says He hates divorce but that he allowed it because of the hardness of our hearts. Or when God wanted to rule the people but allowed them to have a king because they wanted to be like other nations so badly. God allowed these things to be acceptable even if they weren't perfect. I think we learn the perfect will by what Christ chooses to model. Jesus models both a forgiveness that says, "if you confess" and a forgiveness that goes before confession. The model of Jesus on the cross is that He forgave before anyone asks.

Luke 23:33-34
33 And when they came to the place called The Skull, there they crucified Him and the criminals, one on the right and the other on the left. 34 But Jesus was saying, "Father, forgive them; for they do not know what they are doing."

His forgiveness didn't depend on the people. I know this is difficult. We want an apology. We want to believe the person has changed or regrets hurting us. I wanted the person who abused me to apologize and acknowledge the pain he caused. I didn't want him to feel like he was getting away with something, especially since abuse is an intentional act. But it hadn't happened when God was telling me to forgive, and I had to accept that the apology may never come. Many victims of abuse never get apologies and their perpetrators may not feel sorry. But I know it is still possible for forgiveness to happen.

You may be wondering if I got a response to my letter and the answer is yes. He wrote back and apologized. If no one has ever apologized to you, I'd like to tell you that I'm sorry for what happened to you. God is sorry for what happened to you. It was unjustified and unfair. There's nothing that can excuse it. You deserved so much better than what life has given you.

Pray:

God, help me to forgive those who have offended me. Remove any bitterness and anger in my heart. Help me to release the pain. Thank you for forgiving me for every sin. I trust your forgiveness and refuse to walk in condemnation. In Jesus' name, Amen.

Reflect:

Is there someone I need to forgive?

What emotions are my unforgiveness covering up?

Do you have fears associated with forgiveness?

Chapter 10 – Community

Galatians 6:2
2 Bear one another's burdens, and so fulfill the law of Christ.

Scriptures

- ☐ Romans 13:1-4
- ☐ Galatians 6:1-2
- ☐ 1 Corinthians 5:1-5

I wanted to write a chapter that talks about how our community, especially families and churches, can deal with issues of abuse. I've rewritten this chapter numerous times. There are so many questions to consider. Is it theologically sound? Is it too critical or not critical enough? Does it take into account the real trauma of abuse and the genuine belief in the power of God to transform the worst of sinners? Basically, under the worst of circumstances, what could be the best of outcomes?

Too often, I saw the worst outcome. I saw accusations made, and those entrusted with the information didn't believe, created excuses, or chose to ignore it. In most cases, sin was overlooked under the claim of grace, and consequences never happened. The only thing this grace seemed to cost the community was giving up its advocacy for the victim. This was the idea of grace handed to me. Before I read scripture, all I had were the living epistles of my community, and I assumed their lives would match the page. But when we filter the scripture through our fears, the lives others are reading say more about self-preservation than God. Their responses to abuse wrongly labeled a victim's insecurity as humility, silence as sacrifice, and foregoing justice as godly. So, when abuse happened to me, I couldn't imagine how speaking up would make a difference. I thought I had to handle it alone. I decided I would rather stay aside than add on the rejection of being put aside.

But was this really God's grace–a grace that is given as casually as we would ignore someone who forgot to speak or cut us off in traffic? Was grace just how we ask others to excuse our shortcomings or a pass we give to socially acceptable offenses? Was grace just asking for lowered expectations, for a delay in passing judgment until tempers have passed and a confrontation seems unlikely? When these questions were brought to God, and I studied scripture for myself, I came face to face with Jesus on the cross, the pathway that allows us to walk in grace.

And as I learned more about God's grace, about a savior who died so that I could receive that grace, I knew what I saw as a child couldn't be a true reflection of God's grace. How can God's grace give up so much and ours give up so little? God's grace embraces pain for the sake of another. Unfortunately, our idea of grace hides pain to avoid conflict. And that's the first truth I understood about God's grace: the giver must pay the penalty of the offense. Jesus gave his life because death was the cost that justice demanded for sinning. I think it would be transformational to see our communities risk their reputations and comfort to deal openly and honestly with abuse in a way that leads to healing. If our communities modeled God's grace, we'd share in the survivor's sorrow, we'd talk about abuse public, so it doesn't have to whispered in corners. We would model standing in pain without shame. We would take on as much as we could even if it's impossible to take on everything.

The second lesson I realized was Jesus had a choice in giving grace. He could have refused. When we pressure victims into silence, into handling it the way that we think they should, we continue to victimize them by forcing another act on them. True mercy can only come from the person that's been offended. The opportunity to show mercy is an agency that victims should be empowered to embrace or reject. Whether they want to press charges, disclose identities, or handle it in a personal way, is up to them. We need the courage to stand with victims and trust God with the outcomes. God is a God of justice and has given us governments and judicial systems as gifts. He even refers to them as "ministers for our good" (Romans 13:1-4). I say this because there are some who view taking issues outside of the home or the church as a betrayal, but God is everywhere and working in ways we don't always understand. We must admit that our churches and families aren't equipped to handle everything.

The last thing I realized about grace is its goal is reconciliation with God. This helped me understand that justice can be a form of grace. If it takes punishment, separation, or other consequences for offenders to find their way back to God, then there's grace in every step of it.

Staying reconciled to God and to communities can be hard for abuse survivors. The worst fears we have about our abusers are now placed on everyone we know. So the consistency of communities to show love and concern can move us towards God instead of away from Him. There is no underestimating the power of being continually loved even when you are resisting it at every turn.

Providing refuge is showing love. Communities can do their best to offer safety. We can help the vulnerable feel defended and protected. A community can't pay the victim back for what has happened to them; they can put in place restrictions that safeguard the abused from future harm. For churches, it may mean policy updates. For families, it may mean a breaking of relationship. For all, there's a sense of separation, of restrictions, creating a safe place to grieve and heal.

And maybe I should have started here, but if we can do none of these things, if we lack the courage to confront, defend, or to submit to the justice of every form, I think the least we can do is admit there is a need for grace, mercy and justice because abuse is sin. We can admit that abuse is unequivocally wrong, that nothing excuses it. Just having a church, family, or community agree completely on this point could create a foundation to look more like God, to stand apart in a world and be defined by our love like the word suggests. Abuse is wicked even when there's no police report, no hospital room, no physical injury, or no recent event.

What will it take for us to recognize how awful it is? Are we waiting for dead bodies, suicide, or depression? Are we judging by age or whether it was violent? When will we say that it all is too much? If we never know the depths of a victim's pain, if we can't see how it'll affect their lives, all we can be sure of is that God hates when the weak are taken advantage of. Abuse is an abomination to Him. He hates violence and sexual immorality. God destroyed nations for it, and the tribes of the Israelites went to war over it.

Even in the New Testament, when Paul hears about sexual immorality, he states the church should be mourning (1 Corinthians 5:1-5). The depth of destruction caused by abuse is heartbreaking and damaging to the soul and spirit. We must become unified in recognizing it as entirely wicked. It is evil - not a mistake, not a rough edge, not a temptation that needs time to conquer, or an individual and private problem, but sinful and demonic.

    I believe that God is calling us to greater accountability. Let us not underestimate our influence on those who are watching how we handle hard circumstances. We can no longer set aside a victim's suffering as inconsequential to the well-being of the entire community. Grievances bought against our communities may be hurtful but it's better than the alternative- those victims silently walking away from their faith community and God because they don't think we're worth the conversation.

Pray:

Lord, we repent for not defending those who you have put in our care. We repent for taking your place. We repent for not always having the courage to love in the way you've called us to. Help us to defend the weak, to strengthen them and nurture them along a path that keeps them in your hand. In the name of Jesus, Amen.

Reflect:

What can our communities do to better support victims of abuse?

Afterword

Romans 10:8-11 (NKJV)
8 But what does it say? "The word is near you, in your mouth and in your heart" (that is, the word of faith which we preach): 9 that if you confess with your mouth the Lord Jesus and believe in your heart that God has raised Him from the dead, you will be saved. 10 For with the heart one believes unto righteousness, and with the mouth confession is made unto salvation. 11 For the Scripture says, "Whoever believes on Him will not be put to shame."

Everyday I'm still learning about this journey. This book has been an expansion on a book written over 10 years ago. Since then, I've grown as a woman and minister and felt led to write more. I'll continue writing and invite you to join that journey with me at freeingfaith.com. I have as much to learn as I have to teach.

But whether your journey with me stops here or not, please know there is a part of healing that requires God alone. As victims of abuse, we can relate to stories like Hagar and Tamar, but it doesn't matter if we can't find ourselves in the story of Christ. There are some things books and testimonies can't transfer, some healing only found in the presence of God, some wholeness only found through worship, some truth only believed when God speaks directly to us.

The best thing this book can do is to direct you to God to ask your own questions and find those answers in relationship with Him. If by some chance, you've found yourself at the end of the book and haven't given your life to Jesus Christ, I can't imagine a better time than now. It's been the best decision of my life. I pray that it's yours too.

www.ingramcontent.com/pod-product-compliance
Lightning Source LLC
LaVergne TN
LVHW051834080426
835512LV00018B/2862